KITCHEN CRAFTS

KITCHEN CRAFTS

by **Linda** and **John Cross**

Illustrated by **Burt Blum**
Photographs by **John Retallack**

MACMILLAN PUBLISHING CO., INC.
New York

COLLIER MACMILLAN PUBLISHERS
London

Macmillan Publishing Co., Inc.
866 Third Avenue, New York, N.Y. 10022
Collier-Macmillan Canada Ltd.

First Printing 1974

Library of Congress Cataloging in Publication Data

Cross, Linda.
  Kitchen crafts.

  1. Handicraft. I. Cross, John, 1936- joint author. II. Title.
TT157.C75   745.5   73-8351
ISBN 0-02-528940-3
ISBN 0-02-009430-2 (pbk.)

Printed in the United States of America

For
V. M. S.

CONTENTS

KITCHEN CRAFTS

INTRODUCTION

Maybe the best way to introduce this book is to tell you a little bit about why and how it came about. First the "why."

There must be something like eight million crafts books floating around out there, and some of them are pretty darn good. So we didn't start out with the idea that what the world needed was just some more how-to advice. What we wanted to do was to show people that many of the basic crafts could be explained and executed using raw materials that they have within reach on their kitchen shelves. We're fairly familiar with a lot of craft techniques, and we're on pretty good terms with most of the stuff in our kitchen. We seem to spend so much of our time there. Papier-maché from kitchen flour was probably the original spark for the idea. The list of things we've made with maché is almost endless. And no crafts material is more readily available than flour. Working with what was around had to be the way most crafts began. That's the "why."

The "how" part was the fun part. We did what we hope you'll end up doing once you've had a chance to run through this book. First we had to say, "Okay, we've got this idea about using kitchen ingredients to explain the basics of a lot of good solid crafts; what should we include?" As mentioned above, papier-maché was a good starting point. It's a beautiful craft, involving little more than the cost of a cup of flour. Perfect. What else could we make with flour? What other crafts could we demonstrate? What else? The answers resulted in Chapter 1. What other crafts could we make using kitchen raw materials? What crafts did the ingredients themselves inspire? Pasta?—very pretty shapes. Shell crafts to make. Eggs?—Fabergé made a fortune decorating eggs for the czar. We made another chapter. Nuts? beans?— tie-dyeing. Cans?—tin cutting. Kitchen wax? —candles, batik, wax casting. What crafts could we pass along? What could we use? It was very exciting. And very surprising. It had our imaginations really running. We very much hope it will do the same for yours. Be curious. Then be patient. It will happen.

FLOUR

If flour had no other use than as an ingredient in the glue paste that makes papier-maché it would still be a staple in our kitchen. Papier-maché is poor man's pottery. And it's so simple. Flour, water, last week's newspaper, and you can make just about anything you can think of. The maché recipes we've included are meant to get you started. After that, the list of things to make is almost endless.

But flour does have other uses, some of which are even edible. However, saying gingerbread houses and Christmas tree ornaments are made for eating is like saying thoroughbred racehorses are raised for getting small jockeys from one place to another. The only problem with edible crafts is that an eater might show up. So we've included some inedible dough recipes as well. They're just as pretty and they last longer.

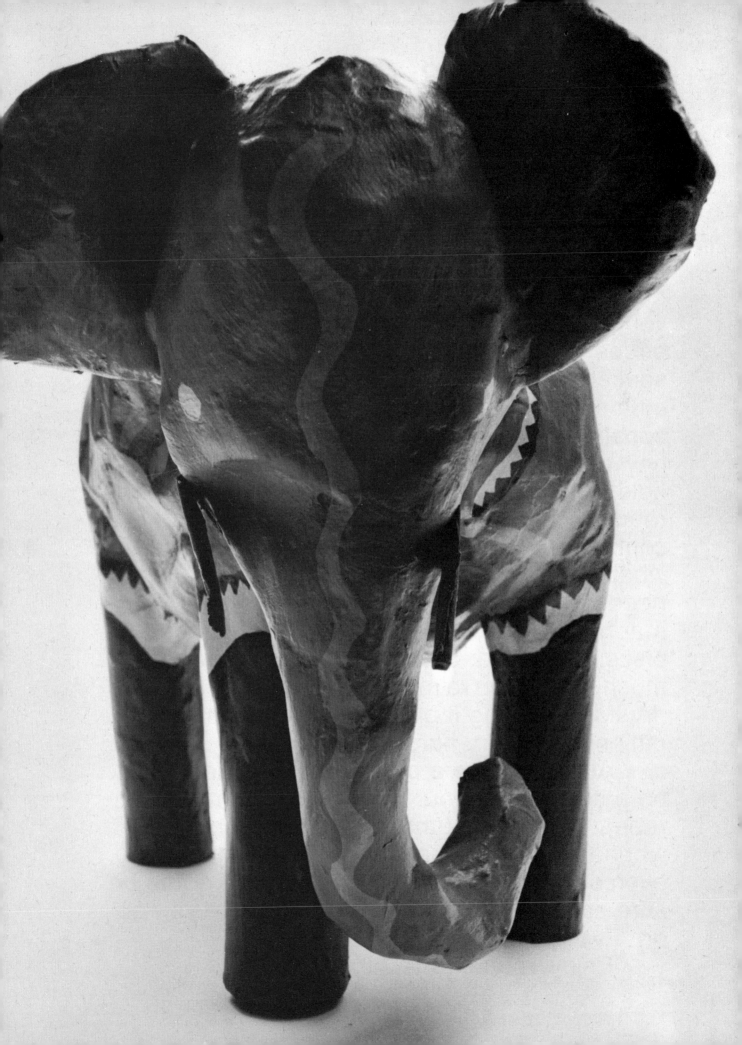

ABOUT PAPIER-MACHÉ

The whole idea of papier-maché is that by mixing plain old everyday kitchen flour with plain old everyday water you get a very simple but very strong glue paste. Maché itself is nothing more than strips of paper glued together with the flour paste. There are lots of different techniques for machéing, but for most things you can use strips of torn newspaper (torn edges seem to blend better than cut ones) soaked in the paste, then wrapped mummy-style around a form you've constructed. Lots of times we use wadded-up newspaper (dry, not machéd) as the basic form held together with masking tape until we're ready to work. Other times we use cans, containers, found objects, sticks, stones, or whatever as the basic shapes. If your shape needs appendages, tape them on before you maché, so that they'll hold on firmly once the piece is finished. Since the work can get pretty mushy while you're machéing, you may have to dry it by hanging it or resting it on its side. Be patient. It will dry hard, very hard.

All crafts take a great deal of patience, so be patient. Take your time. Don't rush. We'll repeat this thought throughout the book whenever we think patience might be needed to overcome anxiety. With maché you've got to be sure each step is completely dry before you go on. Even drier.

Enjoy yourself.

FLOUR-AND-WATER PASTE FOR PAPIER-MACHÉ

Paste
½ cup flour
1 cup water
a dash of white household
   glue
bowl

Add flour gradually to cup of water in bowl and stir with hand until all lumps are gone. Add dash of glue and stir to mix thoroughly.

ADDING FLOUR TO WATER SEEMS TO MAKE A SMOOTHER PASTE.

TO APPLY PAPIER-MACHÉ:

torn (not cut) newspaper
   strips, 1 by 3 inches
flour-and-water paste
   (see above)
form or container to be
   machéd
aluminum foil sheet for
   drying

Dip newspaper strips in flour-and-water paste. Wring out excess by pulling strips through fingers. Prepare adequate supply of strips and keep them handy on edge of bowl.
Apply overlapping layers mummy-style (beginning with undersides or hard-to-reach areas) until surface is completely covered and smooth. For large or complicated pieces, maché difficult areas, and allow to dry overnight before completing process.
For very smooth surface, use tiny strips of soaked paper to patch uneven spots. Let piece dry three to four days (or until absolutely dry).

TO FINISH:

Spackle Solution
3 tbl. dry powdered spackle
½ cup water
bowl
brush
fine sandpaper

Add water to spackle in bowl and mix until smooth. Brush wet spackle solution over dried papier-maché sculpture. *Maché must be absolutely dry or spackle will crack as it dries.* Let spackle dry four to five hours (or until absolutely dry). Sand lightly until rough spots are removed.

BE SURE EACH STEP IS THOROUGHLY DRY.
LET IT DRY ANOTHER DAY.
WITH PAPIER-MACHÉ, PATIENCE IS A VIRTUE.

TO PAINT:

paints
   tempera (clean brush with
   water) or enamel (clean
   brush with turpentine)
brushes
   medium, for background
   fine, for details
clear enamel or plastic spray

For best surface, first paint base coat of white paint. Allow to dry. Paint on background color. Allow to dry. Paint on final design. Allow to dry.
Spray with clear protective coating.

1. TAPE WAD

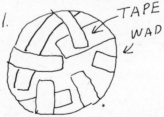
2. DIP NEWSPAPER STRIPS IN FLOUR PASTE

3. APPLY WET STRIPS TO FORM OVERLAPPING TILL SMOOTH. LET DRY.

4. BRUSH ON SPACKLE SOLUTION. DRY. SAND.

5. PAINT

6. SPRAY WITH CLEAR SPRAY.

PAPIER-MACHÉ HAMBURGER

TO FORM HAMBURGER PATTY AND BUN:

2 plastic lids from 1-lb. coffee cans
full sheets of newspaper
masking tape

Wad and tape bunlike mounds of dry newspaper to one side of each lid. Then wad and tape pattylike shape roughly 3½ inches in diameter.

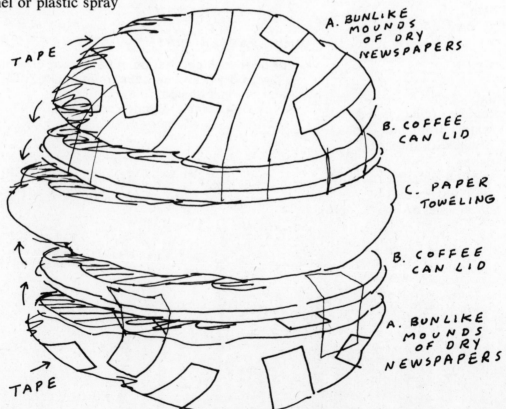

TO MACHÉ:

flour paste (see p. 7)
aluminum foil
paper toweling

Read "About Papier-Maché" (p. 6).
Cover bun halves with maché strips and place flat side down on foil to dry. When dry, spackle, allow to dry, and sand.
To give patty a rough hamburgerlike texture, use paste-soaked strips of paper toweling instead of newspaper strips. Let all pieces dry.

TO PAINT:

tempera paints (white, red, yellow, brown)
water
brushes

Paint hamburger patty brown.
Paint bun light brown (white paint plus dash of brown, dash of yellow).
Allow to dry. Dribble red-paint ketchup on patty.

TO ASSEMBLE:

white household glue
clear enamel or plastic spray

Spread glue on both sides of patty and position between bun sides.
Spray on protective coating.

A. BUNLIKE MOUNDS OF DRY NEWSPAPERS
B. COFFEE CAN LID
C. PAPER TOWELING
B. COFFEE CAN LID
A. BUNLIKE MOUNDS OF DRY NEWSPAPERS

TAPE

8

PAPIER-MACHÉ PIE

TO FORM PIE:

one 9-inch pie pan
full sheets of newspaper
masking tape

To make general shape of pie, fill pie pan with crumpled newspaper, mounded higher in center to resemble baked pie. Tape edges to sides of pan to secure.

TO MACHÉ:

flour paste (see p. 7)
ten 3 by 18-inch newspaper
   strips
scissors

Read "About Papier-Maché" (p. 6).
Cover entire pie and pan with maché strips until smooth.
For plain crust, pinch outer maché edge between thumb and forefinger for fluted effect.
For lattice-strip crust, dip 18-inch strips in flour paste and fold lengthwise to form long thin tubes. Place tubes, seam down, on top of wet pie in criss-cross pattern. Press flat and trim edges of pie with scissors. Add more tubes around outer edge of pie for decorative rim. Pinch between thumb and forefinger for fluted effect.
Allow pie to dry.

TO PAINT:

tempera paints
brush
water
spray aluminum paint
   (optional)
clear enamel or plastic spray

When completely dry, paint entire pie white. Allow to dry.
Tint crust light tan. Paint pan as desired or spray it silver (first protecting pie with newspaper taped around crust edge).
As an option, paint designs on pie crust, such as a cherry with stem and leaf or an apple with stem.
For lattice-strip crust, paint spaces between lattice dark red for berry filling.
Allow to dry.
Spray on protective coating.

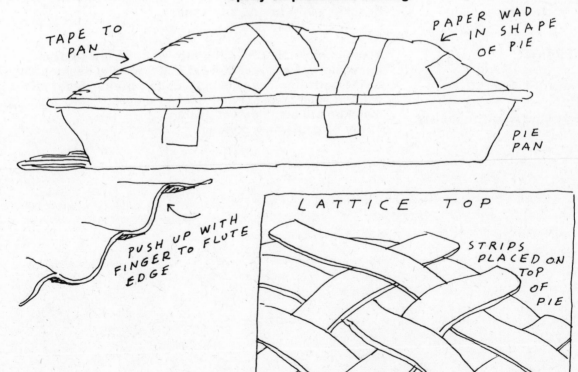

PAPIER-MACHÉ BIRD

TO FORM BIRD:

full sheets of newspaper
masking tape
two pencils

To form bird body, wad and tape dry newspaper into a ball 3½ inches in diameter. Wad and tape a second ball 2 inches in diameter. Position and tape to body to form bird head. Build up neck connection with more paper.
Pinch paper into a point at one end of body to form tail. Tape to hold shape. Pinch paper into a point on head to form beak. Tape to hold shape.
If desired, form wings with triangular wads of paper taped to sides of body.
Insert pencils into underside of body for legs and tape to secure.

TO MACHÉ:

flour paste (See p. 7)

Read "About Papier-Maché" (p.6).
Cover form with maché strips and allow to dry. Spackle, allow to dry, and sand.

FOR FREE-STANDING BIRD:

eight pieces of flexible wire
  3 inches long
wire cutters

To make self-supporting bird's feet, wind four pieces of wire around end of each pencil. Tape to secure.
Spread wires to form three front prongs plus a balancing back prong. Stand bird upright and adjust wires to balance.
Cover wire and pencil with maché strips and allow to dry. Spackle, allow to dry, and sand.

TO MOUNT BIRD ON BASE:

one kitchen matchbox
dry beans

For matchbox base, fill box with dry beans and tape shut. Gently force pencil legs through top center of box and tape to secure bird in upright position.
Cover box and legs with maché strips and allow to dry. Spackle, allow to dry, and sand.

TO PAINT:

tempera paints
brushes
clear enamel or plastic spray

When completely dry, paint bird white. Allow to dry. Decorate with painted flowers and freehand designs. Or divide body into areas (wings, collar, breast, face) and paint in solid colors. Paint beak and eyes. Paint matchbox to complement design.
Spray on protective coating.

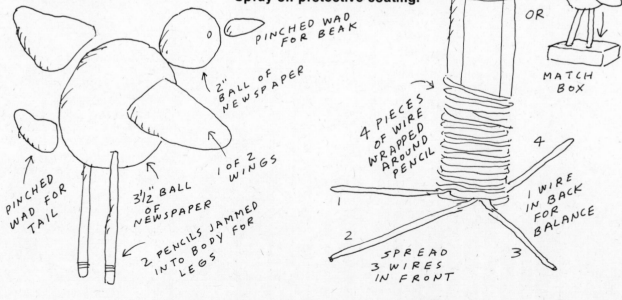

PAPIER-MACHÉ ELEPHANT

TO FORM ELEPHANT:

one 1-lb. coffee can
four pieces of cardboard
    toweling tubes, each 6
    inches long
full sheets of newspaper
masking tape
cardboard
matchsticks

Tape four cardboard toweling tubes in position to serve as legs on coffee-can body. Adjust tubes to balance.
To form head, wad and tape dry newspaper into 3-inch ball. Tape to end of coffee-can body and build up connection with more paper. Cut oval cardboard ears (2 by 1 inches) and tape to sides of head.
For trunk, wad and tape dry newspaper into curved tube and tape to underside of head. Tape on matchsticks for tusks and tail.
Adjust all parts until form resembles elephant shape.

TO MACHÉ:

flour paste (see p. 7)

Read "About Papier-Maché" (p. 6).
Cover entire form with maché strips, beginning with underside and legs. If necessary, maché one section first and allow to dry. Then continue to next section until form is completely covered. Allow to dry.
Spackle, allow to dry, and sand.

TO PAINT:

tempera paints
brushes
clear enamel or plastic spray

When completely dry, paint entire elephant white. Allow to dry.
Paint elephant with freehand designs, or divide elephant into areas (head, legs, trunk, body, tusks) and paint in solid colors. Paint on eyes.
Spray on protective coating.

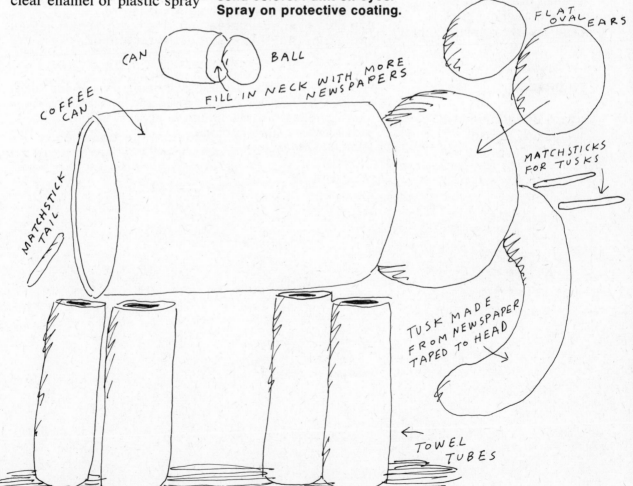

CAN   BALL   FLAT OVAL EARS

FILL IN NECK WITH MORE NEWSPAPERS

COFFEE CAN

MATCHSTICKS FOR TUSKS

MATCHSTICK TAIL

TUSK MADE FROM NEWSPAPER TAPED TO HEAD

TOWEL TUBES

11

PAPIER-MACHÉ DOLL

TO FORM DOLL:

full sheets of newspaper
three 6-inch lengths of cardboard toweling tube
masking tape
cardboard
scissors

To form head and neck, wad and tape dry newspaper into a 4-inch diameter ball around one end of cardboard tube. Tape on small wad of dry newspaper for nose.
For body, wad and tape dry newspaper around neck tube into oblong body-shaped ball about 6 inches long.
Roll and tape dry newspaper into 1 by 4-inch tubes and tape to body as arms.
Tape two 6-inch cardboard tubes to body for legs. Cut two 3-inch ovals from cardboard and tape to bottoms of legs for feet. Fill out with dry newspaper and tape to form shoes.
Stand doll upright and adjust to balance.

TO MACHÉ:

flour paste (see p. 7)

Read "About Papier-Maché" (p. 6).
Cover entire doll with maché strips until smooth. Allow to dry. Spackle, allow to dry, and sand.

TO PAINT:

tempera paints
brushes
2 small black buttons
white household glue
clear enamel or plastic spray
yarn

When completely dry, paint entire doll white. Allow to dry. Paint entire doll flesh color (white paint plus dash of red, dash of yellow, dash of brown to darken). Paint shoes and socks. Paint on lips, freckles, eyebrows.
Glue on button eyes and allow to dry.
Spray on protective coating. Allow to dry.
Dab glue over scalp area and, beginning at part, lay on yarn strips. Allow to dry and trim for haircut.

TO DRESS:

scraps of cotton fabric
needle and thread
scraps of lace

Fit scraps of cotton against doll and cut front and back bodices. Roll scraps around arms and legs if sleeves and pants are desired. Using cotton scraps, gather skirt around waist. Glue in place.
Trim with lace.

BECAUSE MACHÉ
IS FRAGILE,
THIS IS MORE OF
A LOOK-AT DOLL
THAN A
HUG-IT DOLL.

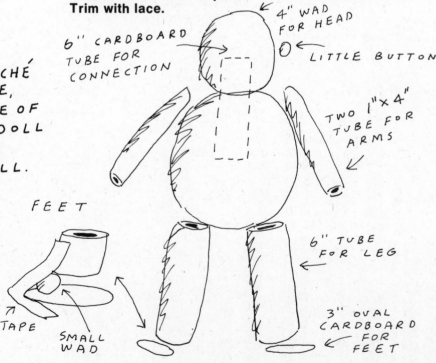

6" CARDBOARD TUBE FOR CONNECTION

4" WAD FOR HEAD

LITTLE BUTTON

TWO 1" x 4" TUBE FOR ARMS

6" TUBE FOR LEG

3" OVAL CARDBOARD FOR FEET

FEET

TAPE

SMALL WAD

MACHÉ-HEAD RAG DOLL

TO FORM DOLL HEAD:

full sheets of newspaper
one 6-inch length of card-
    board toweling tube
masking tape

To form head and neck, wad and tape dry newspaper into a 4-inch diameter ball around one end of cardboard tube. Tape on small wad of dry newspaper for nose.

TO MACHÉ:

flour paste (see p. 7)

Read "About Papier-Maché" (p. 6).
Cover head and neck with maché strips until smooth. Allow to dry.
Spackle, allow to dry, and sand.

TO PAINT:

tempera paints
brushes
2 small black buttons
white household glue
clear enamel or plastic spray
yarn
scissors

When completely dry, paint head white. Allow to dry.
Paint head and neck flesh color (white paint plus dash of red, dash of yellow, dash of brown to darken). Paint on lips, freckles, eyebrows.
Glue on button eyes and allow to dry.
Spray on protective coating. Allow to dry.
Dab glue over scalp area and, beginning at part, lay yarn strips. Allow to dry and trim for haircut.

TO MAKE BODY AND DRESS:

1   pair white athletic socks
cotton for stuffing
needle and thread
scraps of lace

Design your own doll or hand puppet with stuffed stocking body, cotton scraps, or bandana dress.

TO ASSEMBLE:

yarn needle
heavy thread or yarn

Punch needle through fabric-and-maché neck, and stitch to hold head to body.
Cover stitching with collar or dress.

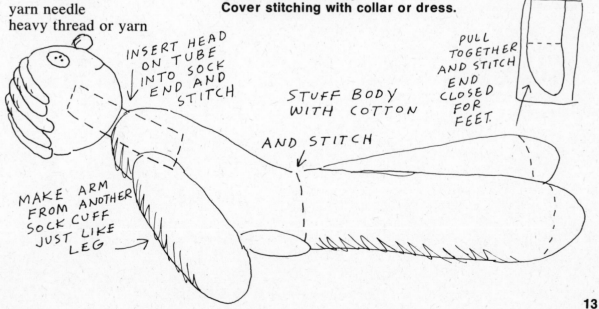

PAPIER-MACHÉ FRUIT

TO FORM FRUIT:

full sheets of newspaper
masking tape
matchsticks

For peaches and plums, wad and tape dry newspaper into 2-inch diameter balls. Insert stick stems and tape to secure.
For apples, wad and tape dry newspaper into 3-inch diameter apple-shaped balls. Insert stick stems and tape to secure.
For bananas, wad and tape dry newspaper into curved banana shapes 6 inches long.
Other fruit shapes can be made by using same technique. Small fruit should be made directly from maché (see below).

TO MACHÉ:

flour paste (see p. 7)
scissors

Read "About Papier-Maché" (p. 6). Cover large fruit (peaches, plums, apples, etc.) with overlapping maché strips until smooth. Allow to dry.
For grapes and cherries, dip small pieces of newspaper into maché and roll into tight 1-inch diameter balls. Arrange grapes into bunches. Insert stems and allow to dry. Leave cherries separate, insert stems, and allow to dry.
For leaves, dip newspaper strips into paste, then stack several layers together. Smooth out excess paste and cut into elliptical leaf shapes. Allow to dry.

TO ARRANGE:

dime-store compote
white household glue

Cover compote completely with maché strips until smooth. Allow to dry.
Arrange maché fruit and leaves in compote when everything is dry. Use glue to hold pieces in compote. Allow to dry.

TO PAINT:

tempera or watercolor paints
brushes
clear enamel or plastic spray

When completely dry, paint fruit and compote white. Tint with appropriately colored paint thinned with lots of water.
Spray on protective coating.

MATCHSTICK STEM

SHAPE OF FRUIT

COMMON LIBRARY
(Flour And Water) PASTE

½ cup regular unsifted flour
1 cup water or more
saucepan
spoon
jar with lid

Place flour in saucepan. Add ½ cup water and mix to smooth paste.
Place saucepan on stove over low heat and add remaining water gradually. Stir constantly until glue thickens (about five minutes).
Add more water if glue is too thick.

THIS IS IDEAL GLUE FOR SCRAPBOOKS, COLLAGES, AND SUCH. YOU CAN'T BEAT IT FOR GLUEING PAPER OR CLOTH.

ABOUT BAKER'S CLAY

Most likely baker's clay got its start as some amateur's cookie recipe that didn't quite work. Some of the ingredients are there—salt, flour, water—but somehow, like a few other efforts we could name, the baked results are as hard as a rock and about half as tasty. But for craftspeople it's a dream. It's much better than cookie dough in that it's permanent, it can be painted, and it's inedible, which is great if you've got a house full of eaters around.

DON'T EAT!!

TO BEST PROTECT BAKER'S CLAY, USE VARNISH OR POLYURETHANE VARNISH FOR FINAL COATING.

BAKER'S CLAY

TO MAKE:

4 cups unsifted regular flour
1 cup salt
1½ cups water
bowl
rolling pin
knife
kitchen utensils for
  pressed patterns

Place flour and salt in a bowl. Add water gradually, mixing with fingers until smooth. If results are too stiff, add more water. Knead with fingers for about five minutes.
Keep clay in a plastic bag if you don't want to use all of it right away.
Roll dough out with rolling pin and cut desired shapes with wet knife or form with fingers. To join several pieces, add a dab of water and press together.
Add incised designs and textures with kitchen utensils.

TO BAKE:

cookie sheet or foil
cooling rack

Bake on a foil cookie sheet in a preheated 350-degree oven until hard. Large pieces may take as long as an hour to bake. Allow to cool on rack.
Paint to decorate.
Don't eat.

BAKER'S-CLAY ORNAMENTS

TO FORM ORNAMENTS:

baker's-clay recipe (above)
rolling pin
cookie cutters, knife, fork
  jar lids, kitchen utensils
  for shaping
plastic straw
cookie sheet

Read "About Baker's Clay" (p. 16). Roll out dough in a sheet to a thickness of ¼ inch or more.
Cut ornament shapes with cookie cutters, jar lids, or wet knife. Incise designs into ornaments with kitchen utensils.
To allow ornament to hang, pierce a hole ½ inch below top with plastic straw.

TO BAKE:

cooling rack

Bake in preheated 350-degree oven for ten minutes or until hard. Heating time varies with size and thickness. Cool on rack.

TO DECORATE:

tempera paints
brushes
masking tape
clear enamel or plastic spray
thread or embroidery floss

Paint ornaments with bright colors. Use masking tape for stripes and patterns.
Spray on protective coating.
Hang ornaments with floss or thread.

BAKER'S-CLAY WREATH

TO FORM WREATH:

baker's-clay recipe (see p. 17)
rolling pin
aluminum foil
knife
1 piece of wire 6 inches long
matchstick
ruler

Read "About Baker's Clay" (p. 16).
On foil, roll out a little more than half the dough up to ⅝-inch thick. Use a wet knife to trim a circle 9 inches in diameter.
Cut out of the center a circle about 3½ inches in diameter to form basic wreath shape.
Loop a piece of wire around matchstick and bury in wreath, leaving wire loop exposed for hanger.

TO DECORATE WREATH:

walnuts, pinecones, nuts, cloves, cinnamon sticks, whole nutmeg, etc.

Imbed nuts and other decorative objects in wreath and secure by overlaying ½-inch-thick ropes of dough. Wad bits of dough into balls slightly smaller than walnuts and taper at one end to form pear shapes. Attach pears to wreath by moistening with water. Shape and add other fruit forms the same way.
For leaves, roll out remaining dough into a ¼-inch sheet. With a wet knife, cut elliptical leaf shapes about 2 inches long. Incise center leaf vein with knife. Attach leaves, moistened with water, to fill out wreath decoration.

TO BAKE:

cooling rack
clear enamel or plastic spray

Place wreath on foil in preheated 350-degree oven. Bake for one hour, then turn wreath over and continue to bake until completely hard.
Allow to cool on rack.
Spray on protective coating.

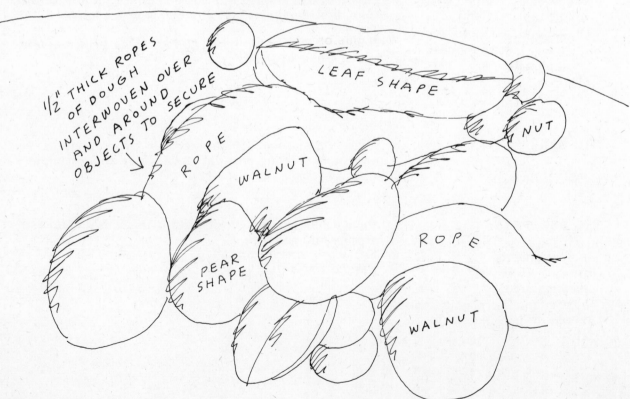

BAKER'S-CLAY BASKET

**TO FORM BASKET,
HANDLE, AND
DECORATIONS:**

baker's-clay recipe (see p. 17)
1 cottage-cheese container,
    4 inches in diameter
aluminum foil
4 pieces of wire 3 inches long
cookie sheet
knife

Read "About Baker's Clay" (p. 16).
To make mold for basket, press wadded aluminum foil firmly inside cheese container until full. Remove molded foil form and place upside down on cookie sheet.
Divide more than half the baker's clay into twelve equal portions. Roll each into a rope ½-inch thick by 14 inches long. Loop ropes around foil form, starting at bottom of form. Break off any excess. Coil rope around top of form to complete inverted basket shape. With wet knife, notch ropes in checkerboard fashion to suggest basket weave.
To form handle, twist two ropes together and shape on cookie sheet into looped handle with open end to match width of basket top. With thumb, make indentation on basket rim where handle will be attached. Insert 3-inch wires through each end of handle (running in same direction as loop) and through both sides of basket rim just below indented area. (These wires will be twisted together after baking to connect handle and basket.)
From remaining clay, shape flowers, berries, leaves, etc., to trim basket rim (see p. 20). Vein leaves with wet knife. Decorations should be attached to basket after baking.

TO BAKE:

cooling rack

Place basket, handle, and decorations on cookie sheet in preheated 350-degree oven. All pieces should bake until completely hard. Check handle and small pieces after forty-five minutes. Remove when hard.
Remove foil form from basket and continue to bake basket until completely hard (about two hours more). Allow to cool on rack.

TO ASSEMBLE:

white household glue
scissors

Dab glue on handle ends and indented rim spots and fit snugly. Twist wires together. Clip loose ends. Prop if necessary.
Allow to dry.

TO DECORATE:

tempera paints
brush
clear enamel or plastic spray

Glue flowers, berries, and leaves to cover wires at handle joint, and trim basket rim. Paint flowers in bold red, white, and green. Leave basket and handle natural baker's-clay color.
Allow to dry.
Spray on clear protective coating.

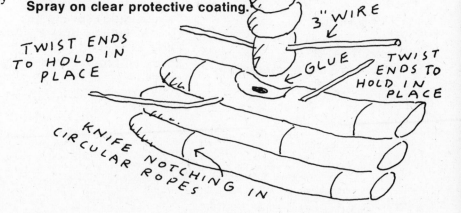

AFTER ALL IS SAID AND DONE, WHATEVER YOU DO, DON'T LIFT IT UP BY THE HANDLE.

TWIST ENDS TO HOLD IN PLACE

3" WIRE

GLUE

TWIST ENDS TO HOLD IN PLACE

KNIFE NOTCHING IN CIRCULAR ROPES

YOUR BAKER'S-CLAY
FAMILY PLAQUE

TO FORM PLAQUE:

baker's-clay recipe (see p. 17)
rolling pin
aluminum foil
knife
ruler
cookie sheet
hairpin or paper clip

Read "About Baker's Clay" (p. 16). On foil, roll out more than half the clay ½-inch thick. With wet knife, cut rectangle 8 by 9 inches and place on cookie sheet. Save balance of rolled-out clay for leaves. For hanger, insert hairpin or paper clip in back of plaque.

TO DECORATE PLAQUE:

garlic press
kitchen utensils for
   incised patterns

Divide balance of clay into four roughly equal parts to use for forming trees and adult figures. Our plaque pictures the two of us and our son. When you work out your own design, divide clay according to the size of your family.

For each *tree* divide one part in half and roll into ropes ⅜-inch in diameter. Twist ropes together to form tree trunk, leaving all ends loose. Moisten plaque with water for better adherence, and position trees on plaque as desired. Arrange rope ends to form roots and branches. For *figures* select position on plaque and moisten. Shape balls for heads, and ropes for arms and legs, and place on plaque as stick figures. Dress them with extra clay pressed flat and cut for clothing. Suit clothes to individuals in your personalized plaque. Squeeze clay through garlic press for hair. From rolled-out clay, cut elliptical *leaf* shapes ½-inch long, and place on tree branches. Fill empty spaces with children, pets, flowers, and other personalized objects. Build *children* using same stick-figure process.

Shape *flowers,* using tiny ball for center with pear-shaped petals all around. For *animals,* roll oblong body and add ball for head, then rope legs and tail. Pinch bits of clay to make pointed ears. For *bees* and *butterflies,* roll oblong body, then add wings shaped by fingers and trimmed by knife. Make *strawberries* by wadding a ball slightly pointed at one end. Pinch three tiny bits of clay *for pointed leaves* to add to top. Dot with fork. Incise center leaf veins with knife, and add other incised patterns.

TO BAKE:

cooling rack
clear enamel or plastic spray

Bake plaque in preheated 350-degree oven. Bake for one hour or until completely hard.
Allow to cool on rack.
Spray on protective coating.

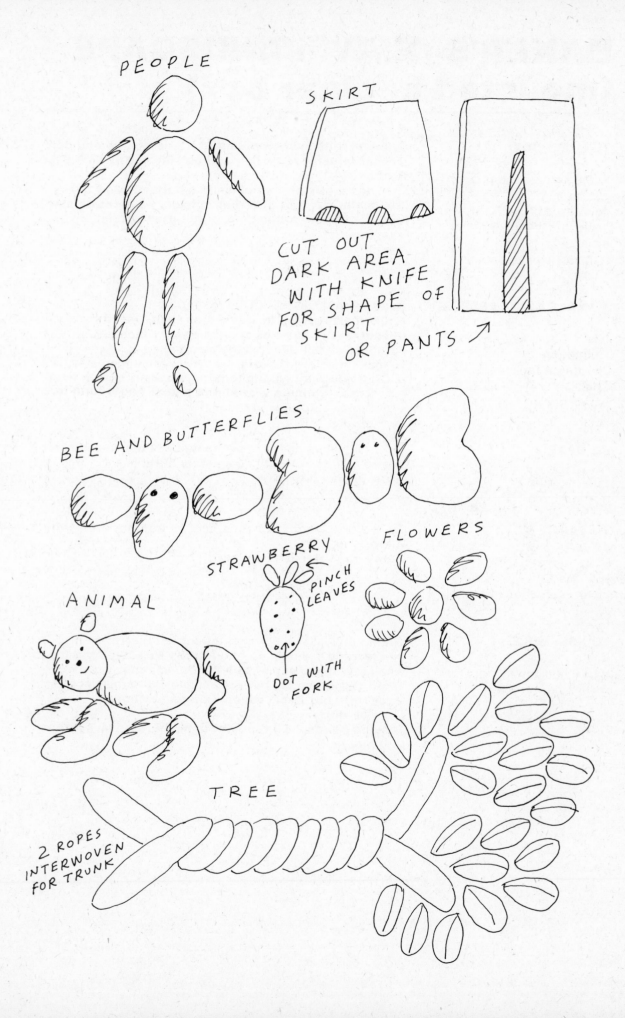

PEOPLE

SKIRT

CUT OUT
DARK AREA
WITH KNIFE
FOR SHAPE OF
SKIRT
OR PANTS ↗

BEE AND BUTTERFLIES

STRAWBERRY

PINCH
LEAVES

FLOWERS

ANIMAL

DOT WITH
FORK

TREE

2 ROPES
INTERWOVEN
FOR TRUNK

BAKER'S-CLAY LANDSCAPE
(mounted in cigar box)

TO PAINT BOX:

wood or cardboard cigar box
shellac
denatured alcohol (to
    clean brush)
brushes
tempera paints

Seal box with solution of one part shellac and one part alcohol. Brush over inside and outside of box and allow to dry.
Give box a primer coat of white paint and allow to dry. Then paint box a bright color outside. Paint inside sky blue, except for bottom; make that grass green.

TO MAKE CLAY LANDSCAPE:

baker's-clay recipe (see p. 17)
rolling pin
aluminum foil
knife
plastic straw

Read "About Baker's Clay" (p. 16).
Roll out clay on foil to a little less than ½-inch thick.
Cut out four or five tree shapes about 6 inches high. Cut out three or four small puffy cloud shapes.
To make animals, flowers, etc., from remaining clay, see p. 20. If you want clouds to hang, pierce a hole in each one ¼ inch from top with end of plastic straw.

TO BAKE:

cooling rack

Bake all pieces on foil in preheated 350-degree oven for fifteen minutes or until completely hard.
Allow to cool on rack.

TO PAINT:

tempera paints
brushes
clear enamel or plastic spray

Paint trees, clouds, animals, etc., in appropriate colors.
Allow to dry.
Spray on protective coating.

TO ASSEMBLE:

white household glue
scraps of styrofoam
scissors
thread
tacks

When all pieces are decorated and dry, arrange in painted and dry box. To make trees stand upright, glue small styrofoam supports behind each one.
When glue is dry, lay box flat and glue all small pieces to trees or to box back, except hanging clouds.
Let glue dry.
To hang clouds, tie thread through hole, then tack thread to top of box.

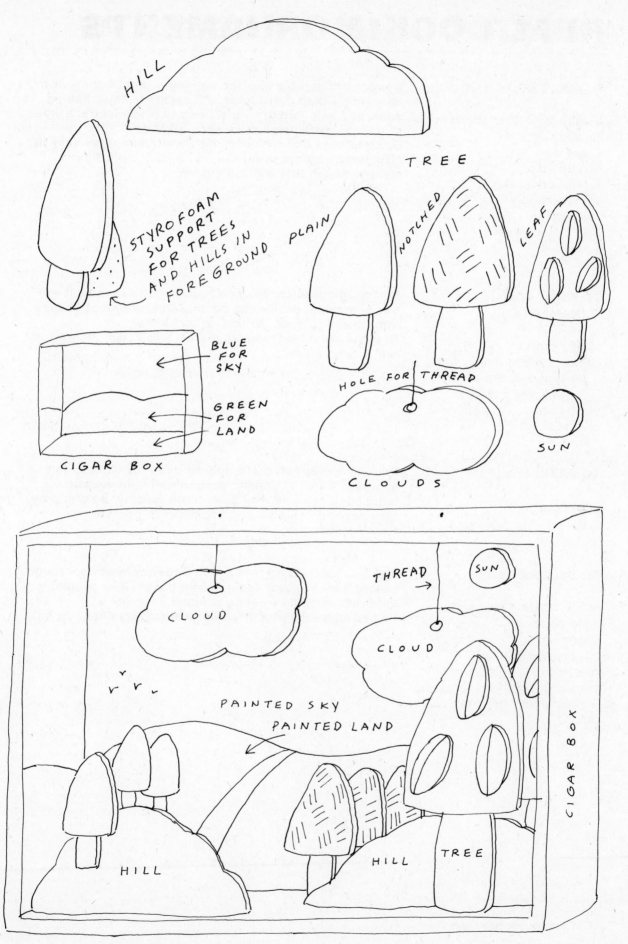

REAL COOKIE ORNAMENTS

TO MAKE COOKIE DOUGH:*

⅓ cup vegetable shortening
⅓ cup sugar
1 egg
⅔ cup honey
1 tsp. lemon flavoring
approximately 3 cups sifted
   all-purpose flour
1 tsp. baking soda
1 tsp. salt

Combine vegetable shortening, sugar, egg, honey, and flavoring. Blend thoroughly. Sift together flour, baking soda, and salt. Add dry ingredients to first mixture, a little at a time, mixing well after each addition.
Since honeys absorb flours differently and eggs vary in size, it may be necessary to add a little more flour to make a dough that will roll out well.

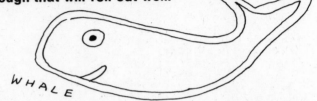

WHALE

**TO FORM COOKIE
ORNAMENTS:**

rolling pin
cookie cutters, knife, fork,
   jar lids, kitchen utensils
   for shaping
plastic straw
cookie sheet

Roll dough to thickness of about ¼ inch or more; it will rise somewhat during the baking. Cut ornament shapes with cookie cutters, jar lids, or wet knife.
To allow ornament to hang, pierce hole ½ inch below top with plastic straw.

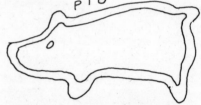

PIG

BIRD

TO BAKE:

cooling rack

Bake in a preheated 375-degree oven for eight to ten minutes. Watch carefully; second and subsequent batches of cookies may bake more quickly. Baking time also depends on size and thickness of cookies.
Cool on rack.

TO DECORATE:

white frosting (see p. 49)
food coloring
spoon
paper cups
pastry tube or small brush
cookie decorations: dragées,
   nonpareils, imperials, etc.
thread

Make tinted frosting (see p. 49). Squeeze frosting through pastry tube or paint designs with brush. Add cookie decorations while frosting is moist.
Hang ornaments with thread or embroidery floss—or eat.

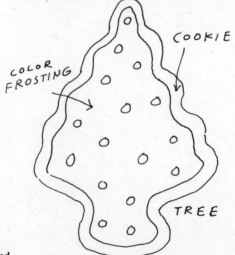

COOKIE

COLOR
FROSTING

TREE

* From the exhibition ''Cookies and Breads: The Baker's Art.'' Recipe courtesy of the Museum of Contemporary Crafts of the American Crafts Council.

BREAD SCULPTURE

**TO MAKE BREAD DOUGH:*

2 tbl. honey
1½ cups lukewarm water
1 pkg. active dry yeast
2 egg whites
1 tbl. salt
¾ cup nonfat dry
   milk solids
1 tbl. corn oil
5 to 6 cups unsifted
   all-purpose flour
2 tsp. cornstarch
⅔ cup cold water
1 tsp. salt
bowl
kitchen towel

Add honey to lukewarm water. Sprinkle yeast over top. Let stand without stirring for one to two minutes. Then stir to blend thoroughly.
Beat egg whites until they hold soft peaks. Stir in salt, milk solids, oil, and yeast mixture. Gradually beat in flour until dough is stiff enough so that it can barely be stirred. Knead on lightly floured board until smooth and elastic. Place in greased bowl and cover with kitchen towel. Allow to rise until double in bulk.

TO SHAPE BREAD:

cookie sheet
knife
pastry brush

Punch down dough and form figure or design with hands, rolling dough into balls or ropes, to be braided and twisted. Build dough sculpture on greased cookie sheet. Use wet knife to incise lines and patterns.
Let bread rise until double in bulk.
Cook cornstarch with water and salt until mixture thickens and becomes clear. Brush this mixture over bread.

TO BAKE:

cooling rack

Bake in a preheated 450-degree oven for ten minutes. Lower heat and bake at 350 degrees for forty-five to fifty minutes or longer, depending on the size and shape of the bread. If the sculptures are small, diminish the baking time.
Put a pan of hot water in the bottom of the oven if you want a more crusty bread.
Let bread cool on a rack.

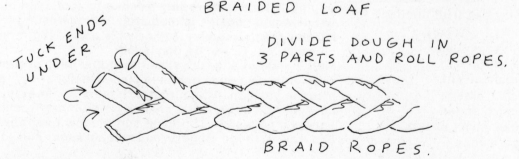

TUCK ENDS UNDER

BRAIDED LOAF

DIVIDE DOUGH IN 3 PARTS AND ROLL ROPES.

BRAID ROPES.

BAKE.

* From the exhibition "Cookies and Breads: The Baker's Art." Recipe courtesy of the Museum of Contemporary Crafts of the American Crafts Council.

GINGERBREAD HOUSE

TO MAKE GINGERBREAD DOUGH:

8 tbl. butter or margarine
1 cup light brown sugar
1 cup dark molasses
1 cup milk
saucepan
wooden spoon
7 cups or more regular flour
1 tbl. bicarbonate of soda
1 tsp. cinnamon
1 tsp. ginger
½ tsp. salt
sifter
large bowl

Melt butter over low heat, then mix in sugar and molasses. Add milk and set aside to cool.
Sift dry ingredients together and beat into liquid mixture about one-third at a time. Add more flour if dough is too sticky to handle. Sprinkle flour over dough and chill overnight.

TO CUT GINGERBREAD-HOUSE PATTERNS:

cardboard
pencil
ruler
scissors
rolling pin
sharp knife
2 cookie sheets
cookie cutters

Cut patterns from cardboard following the measurements in the diagrams on pages 28-29. Knead the dough until smooth. It will be quite stiff. Divide dough in half and roll directly on greased cookie sheets to ¼-inch thick. Dust cardboard patterns lightly with flour, set on dough, and cut all pieces with a knife. Then cut window and door openings. Save door. Cut shutters for windows from scraps. Place these small pieces along edges of sheet for easy removal after seven minutes or so of baking. Re-roll remaining scraps to cut gingerbread men and cookies, or roll long, thin ropes and copy your favorite pretzel shape.

TO BAKE:

Bake in a preheated 350-degree oven for about fifteen minutes. Allow to cool on baking sheet.

TO DECORATE AND ASSEMBLE:

white frosting (see p. 49)
pastry bag with fine-hole tip
knife
candies, cookies for
   decoration
granulated sugar
10-inch skillet
wooden spoon
cookie sheet or tray
sugar cubes

Tint a bit of white frosting to decorate gingerbread men or cookies (see p. 49). Decorate cooled parts of house before assembling and attach them to house with frosting. Put frosting through pastry tube for scrolls and edging. With a knife, apply frosting to roof, imbedding candies and cookies immediately. Allow frosting to harden. Final assembly is done with melted sugar on tray on which house will be displayed.
Melt ½-inch of sugar in skillet over low heat, stirring constantly. Dip ends of house pieces in sugar syrup and place in position. Attach roof with more sugar syrup. Let harden. Add sugar-cube chimney. Add more frosting to seams if necessary. Sprinkle sugar snow over house and tray. Arrange gingerbread men on sugar snowdrifts.

IT'S AN UNDERSTATEMENT TO SAY IT CAN'T BE OVERDONE. A SWEET TOOTH IS MORE TO YOUR ADVANTAGE THAN ARCHITECTURAL KNOW-HOW.

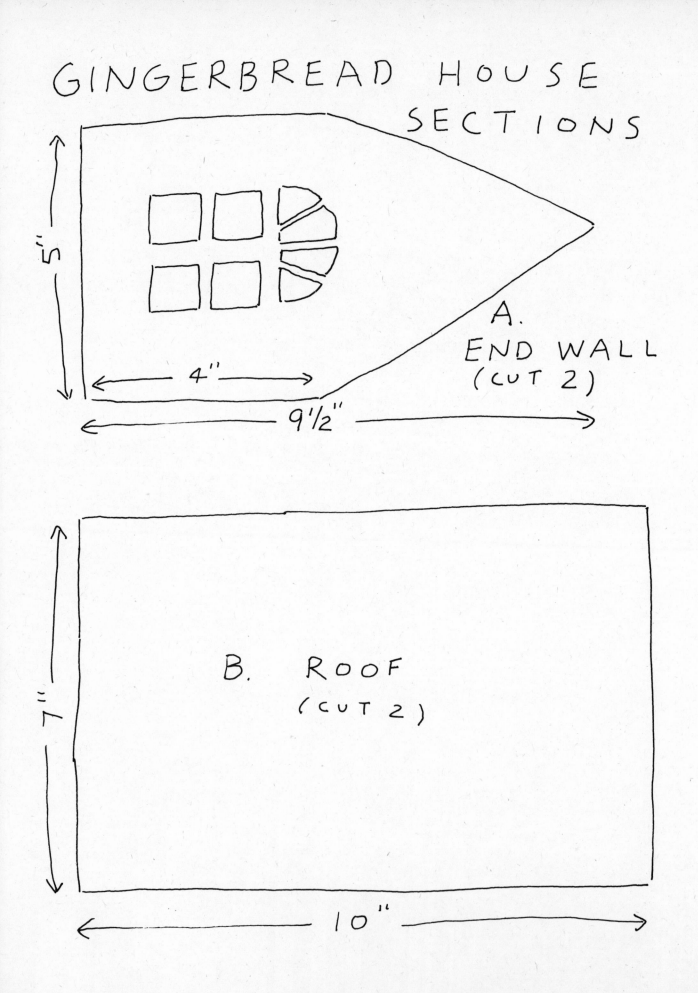

GINGERBREAD HOUSE SECTIONS

5"

4"

9½"

A.
END WALL
(CUT 2)

7"

B. ROOF
(CUT 2)

10"

C. SIDE WALL (CUT 2)

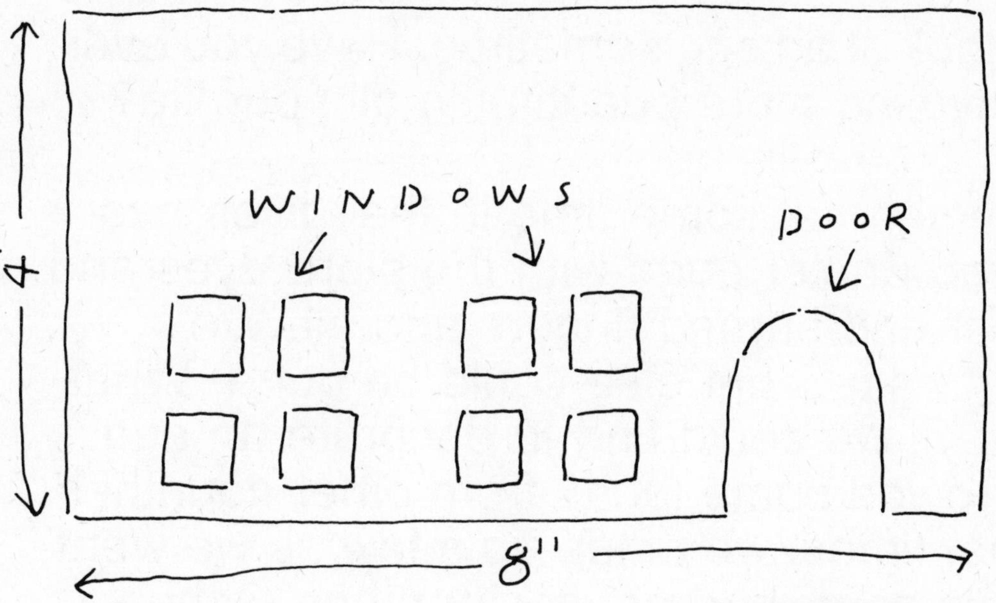

WINDOWS

DOOR

4"

8"

A

B

B

C

C

A

C

EGGS

Take a look at an egg sometime. Have you ever seen anything more beautiful in all your life? Hold on. You will.

Everyone at some time in their lives has decorated Easter eggs with the store dyes and hot water and burned fingers and all. We wanted to see what else could be done. What other ways we could find to decorate an egg. We borrowed some ideas from other countries and other times; we made up a few as we went along; we combined eggs with other kitchen ingredients such as pasta and seeds; we worked with what we had available. And we've really just begun. Almost any technique can be adapted to egg decoration. The Ukrainian way is just like batik, using hot wax and dyes. All kinds of collage materials from your kitchen can be used. Experiment. Have fun. We've found it's best to blow and dry a dozen or so eggs at a time so that you have room for mistakes. Even the mistakes, if crushed into tiny mosaic shell pieces, can be used for egg decorating.

To round out the egg chapter, we've included a recipe for egg tempera, the Italian painters' medium in the fourteenth century.

We've also included one favorite omelet recipe for you to try. If you're going to blow a lot of eggs, we'd suggest you develop a few other recipes of your own. We're firm believers that the best part of the egg is the shell, but you just can't waste all those tasty yolks.

EGGS AND EGGSHELLS

TO BLOW (EMPTY AND DRY) EGGSHELLS:

eggs
darning needle
bowl
saucer of cold water
egg carton

To avoid cracks in shells, allow eggs to reach room temperature before you begin. Pierce small holes at both ends with needle. Rotate needle to help piercing. Make hole at larger end of egg slightly bigger to ease emptying.
Holding egg over bowl, blow into smaller hole. If egg does not empty readily, stick needle into hole to pierce yolk sac. If it still resists, make holes slightly larger. Save insides for cooking.
To rinse inside of egg, suck water into shell, then blow out. Rinse shell under running water, shake out excess water, and dry overnight.
Store in egg carton.

TO REMOVE SPOTS ON SHELLS:

bowl of water
household bleach

Put a few drops of bleach into bowl of water and soak egg until spots are removed.
Allow to dry.

TO STRENGTHEN EGGSHELLS:

white household glue
brush
water

Brush coat of glue, slightly diluted with water, on exterior of shell.
Allow to dry.

TO HANG EGGSHELLS:

blown eggshell
long thin needle
thread or fishing line
button
white household glue

Thread long length of thread or line through button. Thread both ends through needle and draw needle through egg. Dab a bit of glue between button and egg to secure. Loop thread at other end to hang.

TO HANG EGGS WITH RIBBONS:

white household glue
decorative braid or ribbon

Glue braid or ribbon lengthwise around egg. Knot at top for hanging loop.

TO CAST EGGS (PLASTER OR WAX):

unblown egg
vegetable oil
plaster of paris
water
darning needle
wax melted over water

Pierce ½-inch-diameter hole in larger end of egg and empty contents. Coat inside with oil.
Mix plaster according to package instructions, and fill egg with mixture. Allow to dry twenty-four hours. Peel off shell.
For wax egg, substitute melted wax for plaster of paris. Allow to dry twenty-four hours. Peel off shell.
For egg candle, see p. 87.

NATURAL EGG DYES

TO PREPARE DYES:

Read "About Vegetable Dyeing" (pp. 60-61).

Yellow

chamomile tea or
    dandelion blossoms
boiling water
1 tsp. vinegar
pan
strainer

Pour boiling water to cover tea or blossoms. Cover and
let stand about a half hour.
Strain and add vinegar.

Gold

2 tbl. turmeric
2 cups water
1 tsp. vinegar
pan

Simmer turmeric and water for twenty minutes; then add
vinegar. Since turmeric does not dissolve, the coloring
will be slightly marbelized.

Brass-brown

dry outer skins from 8 onions
2 cups water
1 tsp. vinegar
pan
strainer

Place skins in pan of water and simmer until desired
shade is reached.
Strain, and add vinegar.

Lavender-blue

1 cup blueberries or grapes
2 cups water
1 tsp. vinegar
pan
strainer

Crush the berries by hand or in a blender. Add water and
heat to a simmer.
Strain, and add vinegar.

Pale green

mint leaves
boiling water
1 tsp. vinegar
pan
strainer

Proceed as for yellow, substituting mint leaves. Or try
mixing blue and yellow dyes to make green.

TO DYE EGGS:

hard-cooked eggs
pan of hot dye (see above)
slotted spoon
cooling rack for drying

Immerse eggs in dye until desired shade is reached.
Remove from dye with slotted spoon and allow to dry.

MARBELIZED EGGS

TO PREPARE EGGS:

blown eggs
very fine wire or heavy
   thread
long needle
wire basket or dish drainer
   (lined with paper or foil
   for drying rack)

Blow and dry eggs (see p. 32).
Insert wire or thread through holes in egg, leaving long
ends free to tie to drying rack.

TO DYE:

pie pan (lined with aluminum
   foil to keep it clean)
water
paper cup and plastic picnic
   spoon for each color
artist's oil paint or oil
   block-print colors
turpentine or paint thinner
clear enamel or plastic spray

Fill pan with lukewarm water. Squeeze about 1 inch of oil
paint from tube into cup. Mix with a few drops of paint
thinner until paint is the consistency of thick cream.
Carefully drop a spoonful of paint mixture onto pie pan
filled with water so that paint lies on the surface of the
water, but is not immersed. Repeat for each color. Draw a
spoon through the surface of the water to make swirls
and marbelized patterns, but don't stir. The colors will sit
on top, since oil doesn't mix with water.
Hold egg by wire or thread and roll through paint.
Tie egg to drying rack and leave overnight.
Apply clear protective coating.

QUICK CANDLE-DRIP MARBELIZED EGGS

TO PREPARE EGGS:

blown eggs
candle

Blow and dry eggs (see p. 32).
Hold lighted candle over egg and drip random splotches.
Let wax cool.

TO DYE:

dye, tempera paint, or food
   coloring
brush
pan
paper toweling
clear enamel or plastic spray

Brush on dye or coloring and allow to dry.
To remove wax, place egg on absorbent toweling in pan
in preheated 200-degree oven for a few minutes. Wax will
melt to a glossy sheen. Remove egg and wipe off wax
with toweling. Return to oven, heat, and wipe until all wax
is removed.
Brush on second color in random splotches for
marbelized pattern.
Allow to dry.
Apply clear protective coating.

SWISS EASTER EGGS

TO PREPARE EGGS:

raw or blown eggs
spool of white thread
fresh parsley, watercress,
    mint, clover, flowers, etc.
dry loose outer skins of
    common onion
white household glue

Use raw or blown eggs (see p. 32).
Secure thread around equator of egg. Place the leaves or flowers as flat as possible against egg surface and wrap thread around them. Add glue to hold down tiny pieces, (it will dissolve in the hot water.) Continue adding greens and wrapping thread until arrangement is complete.
With same thread, tie a solid coating of three or four layers of onion skins all around egg. Wrap thread securely in snug mesh around egg, then knot.

TO DYE:

pan of boiling water
slotted spoon
clear enamel or plastic spray

Gently lower egg into pan of boiling water, and keeping egg immersed, cook as for hard-cooked eggs—about fifteen minutes.
Remove egg, cool, and unwrap. If you are using blown eggs, blow water out of egg and allow to dry.
Apply clear protective coating.

EGGS WITH YARN STRIPES

TO PREPARE EGGS:

blown eggs

Blow and dry eggs (see p. 32).

TO DECORATE EGGS:

white household glue
scraps of yarn or embroidery
    floss, assorted colors
brush

Brush glue around center of egg; then lay yarn in spiral rows around egg. Glue yarn ends carefully to prevent raveling. As glue begins to set, push yarn together with brush handle in tightly packed, even rows.
Apply glue for each additional row, continuing until egg is covered.
Allow to dry.

JAM-LABEL COLLAGE EGGS

TO PREPARE EGGS:

blown eggs

Blow and dry eggs (see p. 32).

TO DECORATE EGGS:

paper labels, pictures
   from magazines, etc.
white household glue
brush
paper toweling
scissors
clear enamel or plastic spray

Arrange rough placement of cutouts on egg before
glueing. Cut out details from labels, such as berries and
leaves. Brush glue on back of cutout and place on egg.
Press down with paper towel slightly moistened with
water. Continue adding cutouts until design is completed,
wiping up excess glue with the toweling.
Allow to dry.
Apply clear protective coating.

EGGSHELL FLOWERS

TO PREPARE EGGS:

raw eggs
yarn or darning needle
bowl

Pierce holes at either end of egg large enough for pipe
cleaner to push through. Break egg in half over bowl
(reserve contents for cooking).
Rinse shells in cold water and allow to dry.

TO MAKE FLOWERS:

food coloring or watercolor
   paints
brush
green pipe cleaners

Tint outside shells in pastel colors and allow to dry.
Insert pipe cleaner, twisting knot at end to keep shell
from slipping off. Curve stem slightly so eggshell flower
hangs in lily fashion.
Use in bouquet with fresh mint or parsley.

EGGS WITH STRING SCROLLS

TO PREPARE EGGS:

blown eggs

Blow and dry eggs (see p. 32).

TO DECORATE EGGS:

white household glue
brush
toothpick
fine string
paper toweling
scissors
spray paint or enamel
tiny brush
hobby enamel paint in
   contrasting color

Brush coat of glue on half of egg; then lay string on glued area in coils and scrolls, pushing string into place with toothpick. Wipe up excess glue with paper toweling slightly moistened with water. Keep design on one level; don't let string cross over itself.
Allow to dry; then continue design on other side.
Spray egg and string bright color. Allow to dry. With small brush, carefully paint high points of string scrolls in contrasting color.
Allow to dry.

SEED-COLLAGE EGGS

TO PREPARE EGGS:

blown eggs
small-sized pasta and seeds
   (barley, whole black
   pepper, rice, green and yellow
   split peas, tiny noodles,
   whole coriander, fennel
   seeds, etc.)
muffin tin

Blow and dry eggs (see p. 32).
Place each different kind of pasta and seed in a separate section of muffin tin for easy handling.

TO DECORATE EGGS:

eggcup or carton
toothpick
brush
white household glue

Place egg in eggcup and apply coat of glue with brush to first small area to be decorated. Place seeds on glued area; then, with toothpick, move them into desired design. Allow to dry. Continue to shift egg in cup and complete design in same way.
Allow to dry.

TO PAINT (optional):

hobby enamel paints
tiny brush (with a few
   bristles cut away)
clear enamel or plastic spray

To accent the seed collage with color, apply paint with a tiny brush to top only of seed or noodle, leaving the cracks in between natural color.
Allow to dry.
Apply clear protective coating.

ABOUT UKRAINIAN PYSANKY EGGS

What follows is a rather simplified version of a Ukrainian art that was mastered and handed down from generation to generation. Originally, melted wax was applied with a special tool, then the eggs were dyed in specially prepared vegetable dyes. Our recipe is adapted to available tools: a speedball pen, candle wax, and commercial dyes.

The traditional Ukrainian egg designs were loaded with symbolism—fishes, suns, etc. A much simpler design technique is to divide the eggs into sections and fill in the spaces with different linear wax patterns. If this is still too complex, an easier but somewhat cruder shortcut can be tried, using wax crayons instead of a pen and candle wax. The results are fuzzier, far less precise, but ever so much easier. Try both.

THE TRADITIONAL MATERIALS ARE STILL AVAILABLE. YOU CAN ORDER BEESWAX AND A KISTKA, THE STYLUS USED TO APPLY THE WAX, FROM SURMA CO., 11 EAST 7 STREET, NEW YORK, N.Y., 10003. SEND STAMPED, SELF-ADDRESSED ENVELOPE FOR FREE ORDER BLANK.

UKRAINIAN PYSANKY EGGS

TO PREPARE EGGS:

blown eggs
candle
speedball pen with medium
   point (B-3)
pencil
rubberband

Blow and dry eggs (see p. 32).
Light candle and let a pool of wax form at base of wick.
Draw design on egg lightly with pencil, using rubberband
as a guide for lines around egg.
Dip pen into candle flame, then into wax, and draw
design. The lines will remain white. Continue to dip pen
into flame, and then wax, for each stroke. The warm pen
nib will keep wax from congealing.

TO DYE:

food coloring, dye, or
   poster paint
water
brush
paper cup for each color

Since dye is rather transparent, each coat will show
slightly through the next, and slightly alter the color. The
first coat of dye should be the lightest, such as yellow,
and each additional coat progressively darker. Orange
might come after yellow, and then red or violet, and the
darkest color last. Traditionally the last coat was black.
Brush on first color and let it dry. Repeat wax application
before applying second dye. The pen lines you add now
will protect and preserve the first color.
Repeat this process—pen lines in wax, then a coat of
color—for as many layers as desired.

TO REMOVE WAX:

pan
paper toweling
clear enamel or plastic spray

Place egg on absorbent toweling in pan in preheated
200-degree oven for a few minutes. Wax will melt to a
glossy sheen. Remove egg and wipe off wax with
toweling. Return to oven, heat, and wipe until all wax is
removed.
Apply clear protective coating.

DECORATING WITH EGGS

TO PREPARE EGGS:

blown eggs
wires cut 6 inches long
white household glue

Blow and dry eggs (see p. 32).
Insert wires in eggs with a dab of glue, leaving about a
3-inch stem.
Allow to dry.

TO ARRANGE EGGS:

styrofoam ball, wreath,
   or cone
wire
dried foliage, pasta shells,
   spices, pinecones, etc.

Before decorating, tie on wire hanger for ball or wreath.
To cover styrofoam shape with eggs, dip end of each
wire stem into glue and insert in styrofoam, placing eggs
close together until form is completely covered.
Glue added decorations or foliage in empty spaces.

ALPHABET-NOODLE MESSAGES

TO PREPARE EGGS:

blown eggs
alphabet noodles

Blow and dry eggs (see p. 32).
Select alphabet-noodle letters for desired message.

TO DECORATE EGGS:

white household glue
brush
toothpick
paper toweling
spray paint or enamel
tiny brush
hobby enamel paint in
   contrasting color

Brush coat of glue in a line for first row of letters. Place alphabet noodles on glue and move into desired position with toothpick. Repeat process for additional rows. Wipe up excess glue with paper toweling slightly moistened with water.
Let glue dry.
Spray egg and letters bright color. Allow to dry. With small brush, carefully paint top surfaces of letters in contrasting color.
Allow to dry.

EGG TEMPERA

TO PREPARE EGG:

1 egg
paper toweling
jar with lid
sharp knife
oil of wintergreen
   (from drugstore)

Break egg in half and separate yolk from white, keeping the yolk in a half shell. Roll yolk briefly in paper toweling to dry off, then pick up gently with fingers, taking care not to break the skin.
To drain yolk, hold it over a jar and puncture bottom with a knife. Squeeze yolk liquid into jar.
If you plan to keep yolk for a few days, add a few drops of oil of wintergreen for pleasant scent.

TO PREPARE PIGMENTS:

ground color pigments from
   art supply store
distilled water
jars with lids

Add a few drops of water to each color and store in jars, to be mixed with the yolk just before using.

TO PAINT:

palette or aluminum foil
brushes
object to be painted (wood
   or cardboard coated with
   gesso from art supply
   store)

To paint, mix color with a bit of egg yolk on palette. Apply paint with short strokes, letting areas dry before going over them again. Building up several layers creates a translucent surface.

EGGSHELL BOXES OR PEEPHOLES

TO CUT EGGS:

raw eggs
white household glue
brush
pencil
transparent tape
single-edge razor blade

To strengthen shell, brush on coating of glue thinned slightly with water and allow to dry.
Draw desired cutting line with a pencil (around center of shell for box; in a circle or oval on one side for peephole).
Place strips of tape over cutting line, then carefully and gradually make light incisions with razor on pencil line, cutting through both tape and shell. Continue to make small strokes with razor all around line, keeping depth of incision the same until entire seam is nearly cut through. Then make final cut all around.
Open and empty contents of egg.

TO DECORATE EGGS:

toothbrush
tempera or enamel paints
brush
trim, braid, edging, etc.
beads
small cutouts or figures

If you plan to paint the inside of shell, clean out membrane lining by gently scrubbing with toothbrush. Paint shell and allow to dry.
Decorate with edging as desired. For hinges on box, glue on bits of trim. Add bead legs to make box stand.
For peephole eggs, glue braid around shell and make loop at top for hanging.
Design your own peephole scene with miniature cutouts or figures.

CREAM-CHEESE OMELET (serves 4)

TO PREPARE FILLING:

4 oz. cream cheese
¼ cup milk
1 tbl. chopped chives or dill
salt and pepper
small bowl
fork

Let all ingredients reach room temperature. Then, in small bowl, blend cream cheese and milk to a creamy paste. Add fresh chopped chives or dill. Reserve for omelet filling.

TO COOK OMELET:

8 eggs
bowl
fork
omelet pan with 10-inch bottom
2 tbl. butter
oven mitt
heated platter
sliced mushrooms (optional)

Break room-temperature eggs into bowl and mix rapidly with fork until just blended. Put butter in omelet pan over medium-high heat. When butter is hot, but not burned, pour in the eggs. Move the pan and swirl eggs with fork. Pan should be hot enough so that eggs form a light crust and slide around freely in pan. Add cream cheese mixture and continue cooking until eggs are cooked but not hard. Tilt pan over platter, fold omelet in half and let it slide onto platter.
OPTIONAL: For additional garnish, have mushroom slices sautéed in butter until golden.
To make four individual omelets in omelet pan with 7-inch bottom: Prepare as above, using 1 tbl. butter and ½ cup eggs, with 2 heaping tbl. cream-cheese mixture for each serving.

YOUR RECIPES

SUGAR AND SPICE

Because we're working with all kinds of edible kitchen ingredients, the fine line between culinary delights and crafts to be savored by the eye can, at times, become just a bit fuzzy. Maché's a craft. Egg dyeing's a craft. No problem. But a castle made with sugar syrup, graham crackers, and fistsful of candies and cookies has got to end up as a tug of war— should it be gazed upon or gobbled up? Likewise with marzipan. You can eat it, but then you can't look at it. We apologize for the conflict. Maybe you should make two of everything.

Our final sugar thought is all pins. Candy-bar pins, Oreo-cookie pins, whatever-you-love-real-treat pins. Just coat your favorite snack with varnish and pin it on.

Potpourri doesn't arouse the hunger pangs that the sugar treats can, but what it does for your nose is wonderful. There are as many spicy variations as the craftsman can imagine. The original version was made with rose petals gathered on hot dry afternoons, dried, and layered in crocks between perfumed oils and fragrance fixatives, such as powdered orris root, powdered gum benzoin, or gum storax. Most people don't have these items hanging around, but they can be easily ordered from Caswell-Massey* in New York. We've also included a poor man's potpourri, using kitchen spices for those whose roses didn't bloom, and

* For address of Caswell-Massey and those of other suppliers, see "Supplies" at back of book.

a pomander ball, just for the delight of it.
 This is a small chapter, because the nicest
things come in small packages.

COOKIE CASTLE

TO FORM CASTLE:

1 box graham crackers
granulated sugar
10-inch skillet
wooden spoon
knife

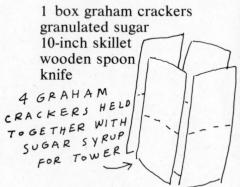

4 GRAHAM CRACKERS HELD TOGETHER WITH SUGAR SYRUP FOR TOWER

Put a ½-inch layer of sugar in a skillet and melt over low heat, stirring constantly to a smooth syrup. Dip graham-cracker ends in syrup and assemble four 4-sided towers for basic module as shown in diagram. Use plenty of sugar syrup, but be careful not to burn your fingers. Then assemble four peaked-roof sections by balancing two cracker squares over a flat square. Score and break cracker pieces to fill triangular ends. Let all pieces harden.
Then, using more sugar syrup, dip bottom of roof and adhere to top for each tower. Let harden.
Don't worry about uneven corners; they can be filled with snowy white frosting and rows of candies.

TO DECORATE:

assorted hard candies and
   cake trim
white frosting (see p. 49)
aluminum foil
pastry bag with fine-hole tip
4 to 6 dozen round cookies
4 ice-cream cones
scissors

Place each section on its side and decorate by attaching candies and trim with blobs of frosting. Squeeze frosting through pastry tube for lines and scrolls.
For windows, cut foil rectangles, and border with frosting and rows of small candies. Let each side harden before setting upright. Decorate only two sides of each tower, as two sides will be interior walls. Decorate rooftops with more frosting imbedded with candies. Let frosting harden. For watchtowers, stack round cookies with icing in between, topped with more icing and a cone roof. Let frosting harden.

TO DISPLAY:

cookie sheet
gumdrops or hard candies
more frosting
granulated sugar

Place sections together on cookie sheet to form square castle with watchtower at each corner. Make a low fence all around edge of cookie sheet with rows of candies and blobs of frosting. Then fill moat with sugar snow.

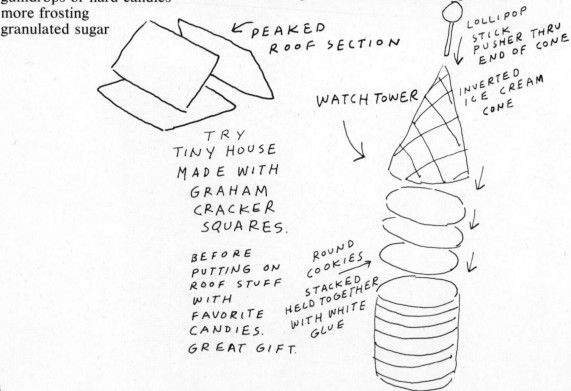

← PEAKED ROOF SECTION

TRY TINY HOUSE MADE WITH GRAHAM CRACKER SQUARES.

BEFORE PUTTING ON ROOF STUFF WITH FAVORITE CANDIES. GREAT GIFT.

WATCH TOWER

LOLLIPOP STICK PUSHER THRU END OF CONE

INVERTED ICE CREAM CONE

ROUND COOKIES STACKED HELD TOGETHER WITH WHITE GLUE

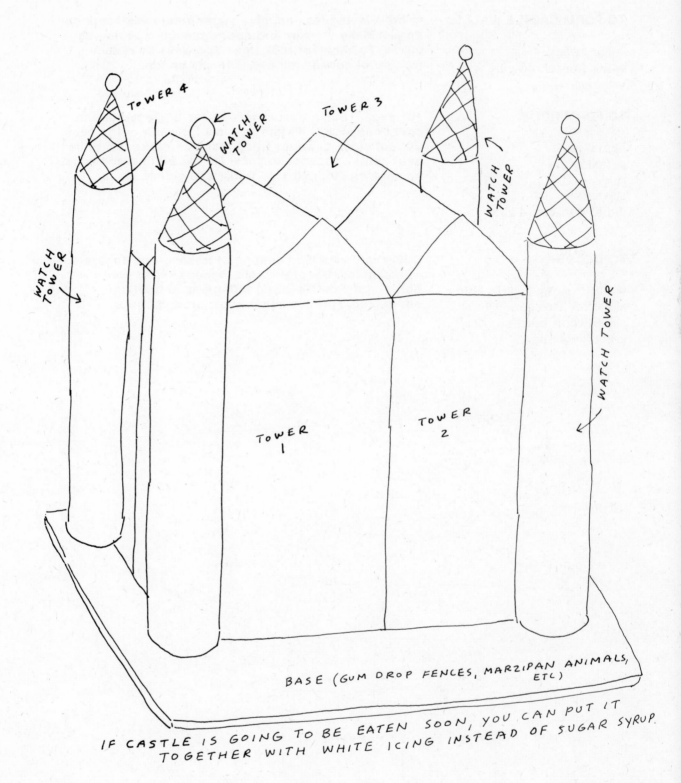

TOWER 4

WATCH TOWER

TOWER 3

WATCH TOWER

WATCH TOWER

WATCH TOWER

TOWER 1

TOWER 2

BASE (GUM DROP FENCES, MARZIPAN ANIMALS, ETC)

IF CASTLE IS GOING TO BE EATEN SOON, YOU CAN PUT IT TOGETHER WITH WHITE ICING INSTEAD OF SUGAR SYRUP.

SUGAR-CUBE CASTLE

TO FORM CASTLE WALLS:

sugar cubes
white household glue

In brick-laying fashion, glue sugar cubes and stack on edges. Make window and door openings by bridging cubes. To allow for roof, peak end walls by reducing number of cubes until only one sits on top.

TO FORM ROOF:

heavy paper
pencil
ruler
scissors
white household glue

For paper roof, measure size of rectangle needed to cover one side, with fold to allow for width of top cube. Cut out piece of paper twice that size. Make two folds near center of paper to allow for full width of top cube, balance on stepped side walls, and glue in place.

TO DECORATE:

white frosting (see p. 49)
assorted hard candies
cake decorations
granulated sugar

Cover roof with light coating of frosting and decorate with candies. Decorate walls, windows, and doors with borders of candies glued with blobs of frosting. For setting, sprinkle sugar snow around house.

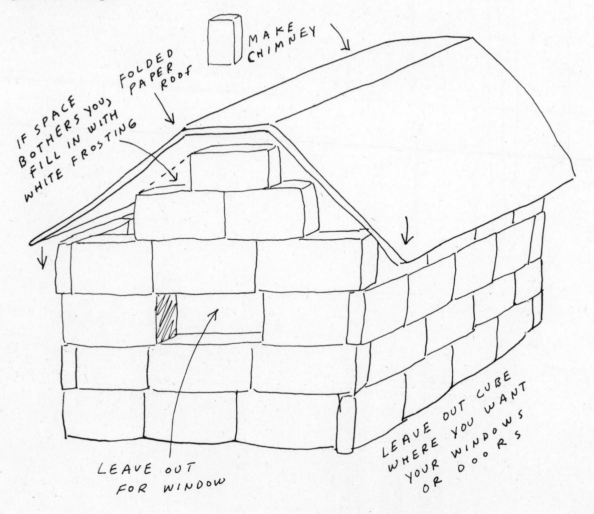

IF SPACE BOTHERS YOU, FILL IN WITH WHITE FROSTING

FOLDED PAPER ROOF

MAKE CHIMNEY

LEAVE OUT FOR WINDOW

LEAVE OUT CUBE WHERE YOU WANT YOUR WINDOWS OR DOORS

MARZIPAN FRUIT

TO MAKE MARZIPAN:

1 cup blanched almonds
   (or 1 cup canned almond
   paste)
1 tsp. almond extract or
   orange juice
2 cups sifted confectioners'
   sugar
1 egg white
bowl
meat grinder or blender
spoon

To grind almonds in meat grinder, put them through three or four times, then mix in extract. If a blender is used, add extract with the nuts to begin the blending. Almonds must be very finely ground. To substitute canned almond paste, proceed with recipe without adding the extract.

Combine almond paste and sugar. Beat egg white slightly and add to almond mixture. Knead until paste is smooth and pliable, adding more sugar if necessary to make paste easy to handle; or, if paste is too thick, add orange juice.

TO FORM MARZIPAN:

food coloring
pastry brush
small brush
paper cups

For fruit, roll marzipan into walnut-sized balls and shape as berries, etc. Or make small animals or figures, as with baker's clay, keeping shapes compact (see p. 20). Brush on food coloring in appropriate colors. For pastel colors, thin coloring slightly with water. Use a small brush to add tiny green leaves or other details. Allow to dry.

WHITE AND TINTED FROSTINGS

White Frosting

1 tsp. lemon juice
2 egg whites
3 cups or more
   confectioners'
   sugar
bowl
electric mixer
damp towel
pastry tube or knife

Mix lemon juice and egg whites in a bowl, then gradually beat in sugar until stiff peaks are formed, adding a little more sugar if necessary. Fill pastry tube about half full with frosting and apply; or use knife. Since frosting hardens quickly, keep what remains in the bowl covered with a damp towel until needed. The frosting will dry very hard and hold candies in place securely.

Tinted Frosting

white frosting (above)
food coloring
paper cups
spoons
small brush (optional)

Place white frosting in a separate cup for each color. Add three or more drops food coloring and mix well. Apply with pastry tube or knife. To apply with brush, thin frosting slightly by gradually stirring in a few drops of water.

ROSE POTPOURRI

TO MAKE:

1 quart dry rose petals
    and buds*
1 tbl. ground orris*
1 tbl. each: ground
    cinnamon, ground cloves,
    allspice, (for a touch of
    citrus: dry lemon peel)
8 to 10 drops oil of rose, oil
    of rose geranium or oil of
    jasmin*

To prepare from your own garden, pick dark red roses on a dry day. Gently pull off petals and dry on rack, or screen away from the sun until crisp—about 2 weeks. Set aside some whole leaves and buds for decoration. When dry, crumble petals and dry ingredients, then add the fragrant oil.

TO AGE:

jar or crock with lid
masking tape
wooden spoon

To age, place mixture in a jar or crock, cover, and seal lid with masking tape. Store crock in cool, dark closet for four weeks, stirring weekly with wooden spoon. Reseal lid tightly after each stirring.

TO DISPLAY:

glass apothecary jar or
    decorative container with
    filigree or open work

Crumble potpourri to be sure it is well mixed. Place whole buds and leaves along inside walls of jar for decorative effect, then pour in potpourri to fill jar or other container.

POOR MAN'S POTPOURRI

1 qt. mixed dried leaves
    (mint, basil, rosemary,
    tarragon, marjoram,
    thyme)
1 tbl. each: ground
    cinnamon, allspice, cloves,
    mace
1 tbl. ground orris*
½ tsp. floral perfume
few drops brandy
jar or crock with lid
masking tape

Prepare Poor Man's Potpourri the same way as rose potpourri, mixing the dried ingredients thoroughly; then stir in the perfume mixed with a few drops of brandy. Seal and store in a jar or crock with lid. Age as for rose potpourri.

* Available from Caswell-Massey. For address, see "Supplies."

CANDY JEWELRY

small candies with paper
    wrappings, jelly beans,
    hard cookies, pretzels
table knife
darning needle and thread
tongs
clear varnish or clear
    polyurethane varnish
turpentine to clean tongs
aluminum foil
pin backs from hobby shop
white household glue
transparent tape
yarn

Use wrapped candies just as they are.
For pins, gently press knife into back of candy or cookie to make indentation for glueing pin back. For jelly-bean ropes and bracelets, string with needle and thread.
Pick up candy with tongs and dip into varnish. Let dry on foil, turning frequently to prevent sticking. When dry, glue pin backs on pins with strip of tape over back for better adherence.
Allow to dry.
Hang pretzel pendants on yarn long enough to go over your head.

SACHET PILLOW

1 tbl. potpourri (see p. 50)
    for small sachet; more
    for large one
scraps: thin fabrics (batiste,
    gingham), narrow eyelet
    edging, ribbons
tiny buttons
soft cotton for stuffing
needle and thread
pins
scissors
paper

To make pattern, fold small piece of paper in half and cut half side of a heart, butterfly, or other symmetrical design.
To make pillow, pin two pieces of fabric with right sides together and cut out pattern. If desired, insert trim or ruffle in seams, then stitch all around, leaving opening for stuffing. Turn right side out.
Stuff sachet, mixing potpourri with stuffing. Stitch opening closed.
Trim with ribbon and buttons.

POMANDER BALL

1 firm orange
2 boxes whole cloves
3 tbl. powdered orris*
1 tbl. each: ground
    cinnamon, allspice,
    nutmeg, ginger
bowl
fork or ice pick
cooling rack
1 yard narrow velvet ribbon
sprig of dried flowers

Mix the ground spices and orris in a bowl. With fork, pierce the skin of the orange all over, making the holes about ¼ inch apart. Roll the orange in the spice bowl. Push a whole clove in each hole until entire skin is covered. Roll again in spice bowl, thoroughly coating ball, then gently shake off excess.
Dry on rack in cool room for two to three weeks. The resultant shrinkage will clamp the cloves tightly in place.
Tie ribbon around orange as you would wrap a gift. Knot twice at top to make loop for hanging. Tie on more ribbon for a bow and a sprig of foliage.

---

* Available from Caswell-Massey. For address, see "Supplies."

FRUITS AND VEGETABLES

One nice thing about working with kitchen ingredients as crafts materials is that you become more aware of how beautiful all these everyday things really are. Maybe if we do nothing more than help you love the beauty of a sliced orange, this book will have been worth your buying.

Two chapters back we fell in love with an egg. Now we're about to start an affair with a split mushroom.

Cut a mushroom down the middle. Look at all those patterns. Now coat the split section with paint. Print it on a piece of paper. The pattern is even more awesome. It's a tree. It's a capitol atop a towering pillar on the Parthenon. It's a beautiful, luscious mushroom cut down the middle. The possibilities of fruit–and vegetable–printing are practically endless. You can use either the raw objects as is, or incise them with your own designs. We've got a few starter ideas, then it's up to you.

What else can you do with fruits and vegetables? If you've ever spilled beet juice on your lap, you've already taken your first step into vegetable dyeing. We hope to help you take the next step. And then there's dried-apple-head faces, and cornhusk dolls, and cornstarch clay, and . . .

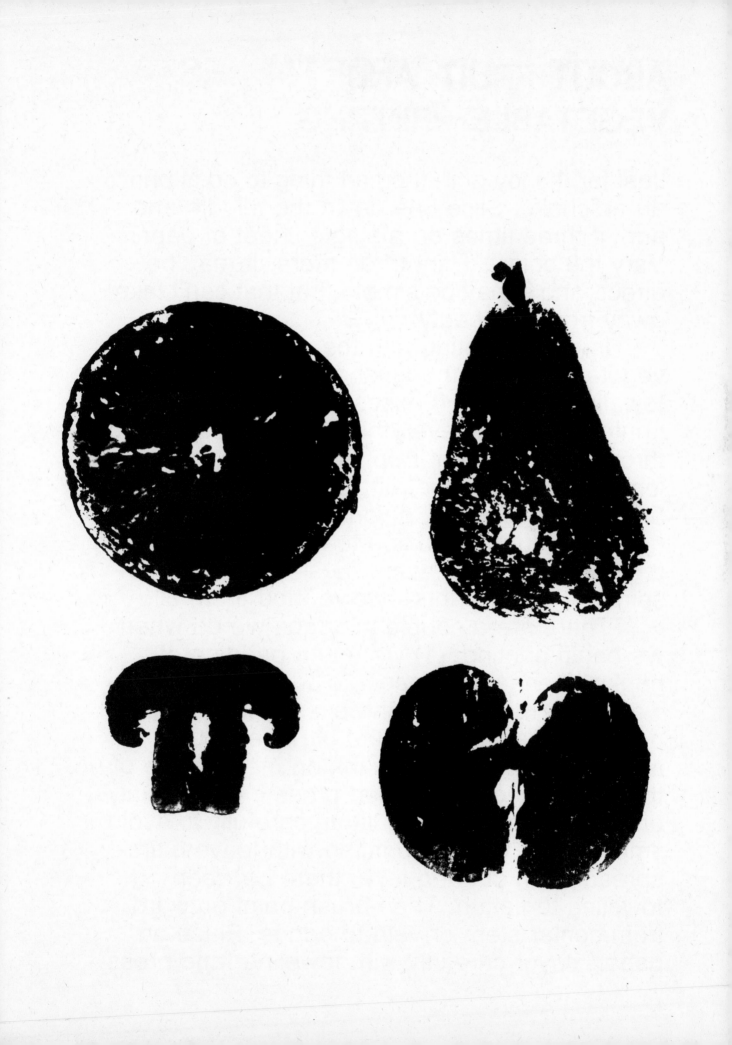

ABOUT FRUIT- AND VEGETABLE-PRINTING

Just for the joy of it, the first thing to do is print an artichoke. Slice one down the middle and print it three times on a single sheet of paper. Vary the colors. Print three more. It may be direct, and it may be simple, but that can't take away from its beauty.

In direct printing, cut the selected fruit or vegetable in half; then place, cut side down, on toweling to drain off excess moisture. We've printed just about everything that's ever passed through our kitchen. Apples, oranges, pears, lemons, limes, grapefruit, berries, artichokes, broccoli, cauliflower, onions (stick a darning needle through the onion to hold the layers together), lettuce leaves, parsley, carrot tops, spinach, houseplants—we've tried them all.

There are a couple of things we do when we begin printing: (1) we use a padding of napkins beneath the paper to be printed, and (2) we usually make about three test prints on scrap paper before we go for the big one. Brush tempera paint or printing ink on the cut side of the fruit or vegetable, then press it down firmly on paper. After printing, lift up carefully to avoid smudging. If you are printing with leaves, first spread them out and layer them between toweling to flatten. Then brush paint outward from center stem or vein to edges. Place on paper, cover carefully with toweling, and press down gently. If you keep your fingers clean and your touch careful, you should be in great shape.

Block printing with vegetables is a lot like linoleum printing, only easier. You need a sharp knife, a couple of potatoes, carrots, or turnips, and a good eye. The eye gets involved in designing the shape or pattern you want to print. Try simple crosshatching or striping. If that works, cut out an animal. Print it. Reshape it. Print again until it looks right to you. Cut away as much of the background as possible. Any raised parts will print. One thing to remember in printing is that your design will be reversed, so unless it's symmetrical, cut it in reverse. If this is a problem—and it can be for letters or numbers—cut a paper pattern, place the flip side of the paper on the vegetable, and cut it out that way. It'll print, right-side right.

One final thought. When you're designing your print, try and work it out so that you can use the same cut shape over and over again. If you're going to cut animal shapes, design with a herd of them in mind or at least a Noah's ark's worth. That's printing ingenuity at work.

DIRECT FRUIT- AND VEGETABLE-PRINTING

For all projects, read "About Fruit- and Vegetable-Printing" (pp. 54-55).

GREENS WREATH WITH BERRIES

watercress and assorted
  greens
cranberries
smooth white paper
tempera paints
flat brush

Work out desired wreath design by placing greens on paper first. Remove, paint greens in shades of olive and green, and print. Highlight design with red berry-half prints.

FRUIT BASKET

assorted fruits and berries
greens
potato
smooth white paper
tempera paints
flat brush

Print basket shape by using crosshatched potato to resemble basket weave. Fill basket with fruit by printing large fruit halves first, in shades of red, yellow, orange. Add berry halves and green leaves. The final design will resemble a Victorian fruit-basket print.

FAMILY TREE

broccoli, cherries, greens,
  or houseplant leaves
pen and ink
smooth white paper
tempera paints
flat brush

Print broccoli stalk in brown or olive for main tree trunk, trimmed if necessary to indicate roots, etc. Add branches, made with smaller broccoli stems. Print red cherry half on tree branches for each member of family. Add leaves to fill out design. Write in names of family with pen.

GREETING CARDS

paper and envelopes
assorted fruits and berries
tempera paints
flat brush

Design your own botanical print cards.

JAM LABELS

gummed mailing labels
assorted fruits and greens
pen
tempera paints
flat brush

Print appropriate fruit half for labels. Decorate with greens. Write name on label with pen, if desired.

Yarn Stripes

Ukrainian Pysanky

Alphabet - Noodle Message

Ukrainian Pysanky

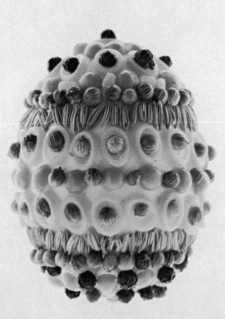

Seed Collage

Tempera Paint

Ukrainian Pysanky

Marbelized

Papier - Maché Elephant

Pasta Seashell Mirror Frame

Vegetable Block Printing with Potato

Hurricane Globe of Pasta Wheels

Tie Dyeing with Nuts, Beans, and Seeds

Gingerbread House with Cookie Trees

VEGETABLE BLOCK PRINTING

CALENDAR

TO LAY OUT:

tablet with smooth white
   paper and spiral binding
pencil
ruler
calendar for reference

On each of twelve pages, draw line about 2 or 3 inches from top to make a margin for name of month and decorative border. Lay out rows of numbers for each month in pencil, using calendar as a guide.

TO CUT LETTERS AND NUMBERS:

unpeeled potatoes
sharp paring knife
potato peeler
paper toweling
pencil
scrap paper
scissors

Read "About Fruit- and Vegetable-Printing" (pp. 54-55). To make patterns for letters and numbers, draw them freehand on a piece of scrap paper the same size as potato half, and cut out. Printing will reverse the letter, so place pattern upside down on cut side of potato. The moisture of the potato will hold the paper in place. Cut out letter in potato, using peeler to scoop out holes. For holidays, cut symbols such as heart for Valentine's Day, tree for Christmas, lighted candle for birthdays, and so on.

TO PRINT:

tempera paints
flat brush
paper napkins
plastic bag

Print with tempera paint by painting raised areas and pressing potato block down on paper (over napkin padding). Remove without smudging.
To use vegetable blocks for more printing, wash and then store in plastic bag in refrigerator.

PRINTING ON FABRIC

TO PRINT FRUIT AND VEGETABLES ON FABRIC:

textile paints from
   art supply store
cotton or linen fabric

First wash and dry fabric to remove soil or sizing. Print with textile paints or inks.
Let dry twenty-four hours.

TO SET COLORS:

iron
paper toweling
newspapers
fabric, decorated and dried

Protect ironing board with newspapers topped by layer of paper toweling (to keep newsprint from rubbing off on fabric). Place fabric face down, then add another layer of paper toweling and newspaper. Press on both sides of fabric with iron heated to 300 degrees, until every inch has been heated, for about three minutes.
Wash printed fabrics by hand in warm water.

ABOUT VEGETABLE DYEING

If we were to really get into the subject of natural dyes, we would be stretching the intent of this book even beyond the loose boundaries we've ascribed to it. It's all much too complex for our purposes, but it is a fascinating subject so we'll pass on a few of our observations.

Before the availability of commercial dyes, all dyes were prepared from locally available ingredients. The nuts, seeds, roots, flowers, vegetables, and even the bugs near at hand set the shades. In actual practice, plants are normally gathered late in the season, when mature. They are then finely chopped, soaked in water and cooked in that same water. Dandelion roots make red-violet, Indian corn makes gray-lavender, onion skins make brass, spinach makes green, parsley yellow green, and so on. We once tie-dyed a white, long-sleeved, old-fashioned undershirt with onion skins and turmeric and it absolutely glows with color.

The catch to all this, however, is that the yarn or material must first be treated to make the color permanent and resistant to soap and sunlight. This is called mordanting, and it is accomplished by cooking the yarn in a special water-and-chemical solution. It prepares the yarn to take and hold the dye. Alum, one of the more common chemicals used in mordanting, is fairly easy to get through your local druggist.

When you really get into the subject, you find that different chemicals affect the colors, as do the metal pans you use to hold the dye. It's all very touchy; no two dye lots come out the same, even when you use the same raw materials.

As we mentioned, vegetable dyeing does get a little bit away from the everyday kitchen craft, but if you end up with a shirt as lovely as ours, it's well worth straying.

VEGETABLE DYEING

TO MORDANT WITH ALUM:

1 lb. wool yarn
3 oz. alum (potassium
   aluminum sulfate or
   potash alum)
1 oz. cream of tartar
5-gal. enamel pan
water
wooden spoon
cup

Dissolve chemicals in a cup of water, then add to the pan with 4 gallons of water. Immerse wet wool and heat to just below boiling point. Simmer gently for one hour, stirring occasionally. Let wool cool in the mordant. Remove wool, dry, and store. Or immerse wet wool in dye.

**ONION-SKIN DYE
(Brass to Brown):**

1 lb. wool yarn (alum
   mordanted)
4 gal. dry outer skins of
   common yellow onion (or
   red skins for darker color)
5-gal. enamel pan
water

Place skins in pan and add just enough water to cover skins. Boil one-half hour. Strain. Immerse wet, mordanted yarn in lukewarm dye, then raise heat and simmer, stirring, for thirty minutes. Remove yarn, rinse, and dry away from sun.

TURMERIC DYE (gold):

1 lb. wool yarn (alum
   mordanted)
8 oz. ground turmeric
5-gal. enamel pan
cheesecloth
string
water

Tie turmeric in cheesecloth bag, leaving room for expansion. Place in 3 gallons of warm water in pan. Soak overnight. Bring bag and water to boil and simmer for two hours. Press liquid from bag and remove from dye. Immerse wet, alum-mordanted wool and simmer thirty minutes.

INSTEAD OF YARN, YOU CAN USE 100% COTTON OR 100% NYLON OR 100% RAYON.

FINGER PAINT

TO MAKE PAINT:

1 heaping tbl. cornstarch
2 tbl. cold water
bowl
spoon
measuring cup
boiling water
paper cup for each color
tempera or poster paints
shelf paper to paint on

Dissolve cornstarch in the cold water. Stir to a paste, adding more cornstarch if necessary. Stir in 1 cup boiling water. Allow to cool and thicken.
Mix a little paint with paste in each paper cup. Or, for small children, use food coloring instead of paint.

APPLE HEADS

TO MAKE APPLE HEAD:

firm Delicious apple
paring knife
rice
whole peppercorns
white household glue
fresh lemon juice
popsicle stick

Peel apple smoothly. Carve features, then insert and glue rice teeth, peppercorn eyes, and popsicle-stick neck. Dip apple in lemon juice and let dry in warm room for about a month.
Features may be further shaped with the fingers as it dries.

TO COMPLETE DOLL:

stocking
stuffing
scraps: fabric, buttons, etc.
thread
glue
cotton for hair

Make body by stuffing stocking around popsicle-stick neck. Add a dab of glue to neck, and tie stocking with thread. Tie thread to indicate waist.
Design your own doll with fabric scraps, etc. Glue on cotton for hair.

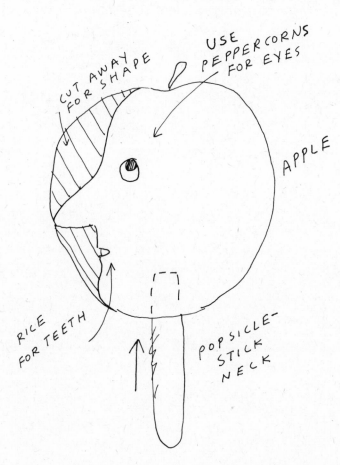

CORNHUSK DOLL

TO SHAPE DOLL:

cornhusks (removed from
    ear and dried in sun)
pan of hot water
tan thread
scissors
hazelnut or bead for head

Soak husks in warm water for about ten minutes or until pliable. Work while husks are wet.

For head and torso, fold a husk over nut and tie at neck; then tie again 1½ inches lower for waist. For arms, roll up slender husk and insert through torso at shoulders. Arm should be about 3 inches long. Tie thread at wrists. To add skirt place narrow ends of twelve husks at waist, overlapping for full skirt. Tie thread at waist, then trim husk ends about ½ inch above waist. Add shawl—a husk slit in half, wrapped around shoulders and crossing in front. Tie at waist again.

TO COMPLETE DOLL:

ruler
straight pins
needle and thread
brown and red felt-tip pens

Pin husks together where they overlap on skirt to prevent curling. Pin arms in desired position. Trim hemline evenly about 5 inches from waist and balance doll to stand.

For hair, soak brown corn silk and place on head. Stitch in desired hair style. For a braided belt, tear husks into narrow strips, tie three together at one end, and braid. Tie around waist.

Let doll dry overnight, then remove pins.

Draw eyes and mouth with pens.

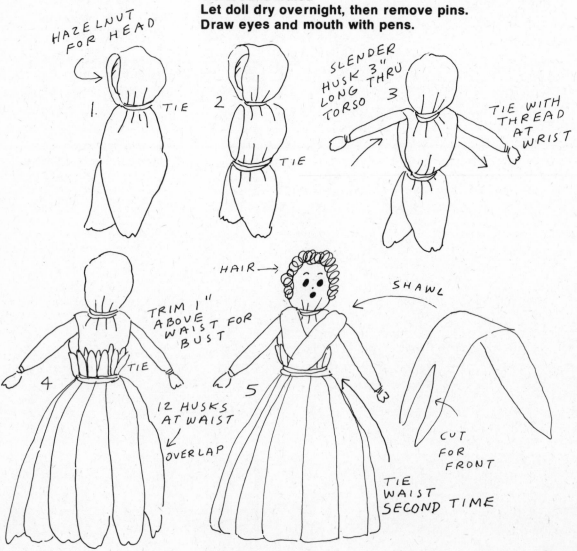

CORNSTARCH-CLAY JEWELRY

TO MAKE CORNSTARCH CLAY:*

1 cup cornstarch
2 cups (1 lb.) baking soda
1¼ cups cold water
whisk
pan
cloth

Whisk cornstarch and baking soda together thoroughly in a saucepan. Add water all at once, and place over medium heat. Stir constantly as mixture thins, then thickens. About four minutes from start of cooking, mixture will turn to a moist mashed-potato consistency. Remove immediately from heat, turn out on a plate, cover with a damp cloth and allow to cool. When easy to handle, knead like dough for a few minutes.

TO FORM DESIGNS:

rolling pin
plastic bag
cookie cutters, lids
wax paper
knife, fork, utensils for
    pressed patterns
paper clips, pin backs
wire
toothpick
white household glue
ribbon or yarn
cooling rack

Roll out clay to ¼-inch thickness on wax paper or store in a tightly closed plastic bag for later use.
Cut with cookie cutters or bottle caps, or mold desired shapes freehand. For raised designs, cut small shapes, moisten with water and press onto larger piece. Etch patterns with utensils.
For hanging pendant or ornaments, insert paper clip for loop at top edge or pierce hole with toothpick. For pins, press wire into back of pin to make indentation. Remove and when dry, glue pin back to design and tape across it. For link belts or bracelets, cut circles or shapes. Insert wire loops in each side large enough for connecting ribbon or yarn. When painted and dry, thread ribbon through loops.
Allow to dry. Thin pieces harden overnight; thicker pieces take longer. While drying on cooling rack, turn pieces occasionally to avoid uneven hardening and cracking. To hasten hardening, place on wire rack in an oven that has been preheated to 350 degrees, then turned off.

TO PAINT:

tempera or watercolor paints
brush
white shellac, clear nail
    polish, clear enamel,
    or plastic spray

Paint with tempera or watercolors. Allow to dry, then finish by applying clear protective glaze.

RIBBON PATH

INSERT WIRE LOOPS WIDE ENOUGH FOR RIBBON TO THREAD.

*Cornstarch Clay recipe courtesy of the makers of Argo cornstarch.

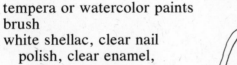

RIBBON LOOPED THRU WIRES

BELT

WIRE

NUTS, BEANS, AND SEEDS

There must be twenty-five different kinds of dried beans sitting out there on your grocer's shelf, at least as many different kinds of nuts, and if you look hard, you'll probably turn up twice that number of dried seeds, particularly in springtime when the gardeners are all going crazy. Even if you do nothing more than randomly scatter them on a page, you've got to come up with a mosaic phantasmagoria. If you're adventurous, the design possibilities are endless.

Beyond mosaics, the very best tie-dyeing with the delicate little designs has traditionally been worked out with nuts, beans, or rice. We'll explain our approach to tie-dyeing. Any way you do it, it's a touch tedious, a lot messy, and the results can be simply sensational.

Finally, we've tossed in a beanbag bug just for fun.

SEED AND BEAN MOSAICS

objects to cover: cardboard, wood panel, box, frame (almost any surface can be covered with mosaic)

assorted dried seeds and beans: chick-peas, coffee beans, kidney beans, lentils, peppercorns, rice, split peas, sunflower seeds, etc.

pencil

white household glue

clear plastic or varnish

brush

turpentine to clean brush

Outline general areas of design with pencil. Then begin by glueing seeds and beans on all outlines. Fill in until entire surface is covered, contrasting light and dark colors. To use very small seeds, such as poppy or celery seeds, make the outline first with larger seeds, then fill area with glue and sprinkle on the small seeds. Press seeds down to imbed them in glue. For sides of boxes or borders try stripes, checkerboard patterns, and so on. Each piece must be glued securely. Allow to dry. Apply clear protective coating.

IF YOU'VE DONE YOUR MOSAIC ON CARDBOARD, PREVENT WARPING BY GLUEING A SHEET OF PAPER ON THE BACK SIDE.

BEAN BEADS AND ROPES

assorted dried beans of contrasting colors: black turtle beans, navy beans, red kidney beans, etc.

hot water

large needle

string

paper toweling

clear enamel or plastic spray (or orange shellac)

brush

denatured alcohol to clean brush

Soak beans in hot water until soft enough for needle to go through. Blot on toweling, then string damp beans. First thread needle with desired length of string (enough to tie and go over head). String beans of contrasting color and shape. Tie ends.

Working while beans are still damp, add small strings of beans for pendants. Thread four or five beans and tie to chain. Allow to dry.

Your own variations will depend on the type of beans available. You might even try connecting links between the pendants for a more elaborate collar.

Spray with clear protective coating or brush on orange shellac for an earthy lustre.

Use same technique for Christmas-tree ropes, using long pieces of string. Try alternating beans with pasta.

NUT WREATH, TREE, OR HANGING BALL

styrofoam wreath, cone, or ball

brown spray paint

walnuts

fine wire

scissors

masking tape

dime-store berries or tiny nuts on wire stems

white household glue

mixed nuts

wide rust-colored velvet ribbon

Spray styrofoam form brown and allow to dry. Carefully break walnuts in half and remove nut. Glue shells back together with short pieces of wire inserted for stems. Tape shell together to dry. When dry, remove tape and insert stems and dime-store berries into styrofoam at equal intervals. Glue on mixed nuts to fill empty spaces until all styrofoam is covered.

For ball or wreath, tie on wire loop for hanging. Trim with velvet bow.

ABOUT TIE-DYEING

Fine examples of this art are available from the Orient, Indonesia, Africa, Europe, and South America. The process is technically quite simple: by protecting certain parts of the cloth before dyeing, you retain the original color of the cloth. In batik, this protection is provided with wax. In tie-dyeing, string, thread, or rubberbands are tightly tied around clusters of the cloth and provide the barrier to the dye. Traditionally, these clusters are formed with a bean, nut, seed, or pea placed under the cloth and tied in position. By varying the size of the bean and the thickness of the tie, you alter the size of the protected area. Bull's-eyes or sunbursts are formed by tying several nuts separated by rubberbands along one long cluster of the cloth. The top bean forms the center of a series of concentric circles dyed with this technique. If more than two colors are desired, you can dip different ties in different dye baths, or you can paint liquid dye directly on portions of the cloth.

Because dye tends to bleed, the color areas will be somewhat fused. However, any protected fold, pleat, or cluster in the cloth will create patterns. The really nice thing about tie-dyeing is that even accidents and mistakes are beautiful. You'll see what we mean.

TO TIE-DYE

TO PREPARE FABRIC:

cotton fabric (old sheets,
    clothing, etc.)

Wash new fabrics to remove any sizing. Work with damp fabric.

TO MAKE DESIGNS:

damp fabric or garment
liquid dyes from dime store
brush
dried beans, peas, nuts, etc.
rubberbands
plastic bags

Read "About Tie-Dyeing" (p. 69).
Divide fabric into sections and design as desired. For bold circles, use rubberbands around large nuts. For delicate spotting, band tiny rubberbands around rice or seeds. Arrange nuts, etc., in stripes or geometric patterns. For bull's-eye or sunburst, use four or five sizes of nuts. First band smallest nut in center, then add the others, one behind the other, gradually increasing size. To add more color to design, paint liquid dye with brush on areas desired. Each nut could be tinted or, in the bull's-eye, each one could be a different color. Then protect from final dye by banding plastic bags over them. To make stripes, simply band fabric at regular intervals. For a more intricate and irregular stripe, try accordion-folding the fabric in about one-inch sections, keeping the fabric in a neat stack, like a folded fan, then banding it at regular intervals.

TO DYE:

dye for background color
rubber gloves
large enamel pan
iron
paper toweling

Follow manufacturer's instructions for dyeing. After dyeing, remove fabric and rinse it under cold water until the water is clear. Remove all nuts, beans, bands, and plastic bags. Dry away from sunlight. Iron out wrinkles, protecting ironing board from wet dye with absorbent paper.
When laundering, use cool water.

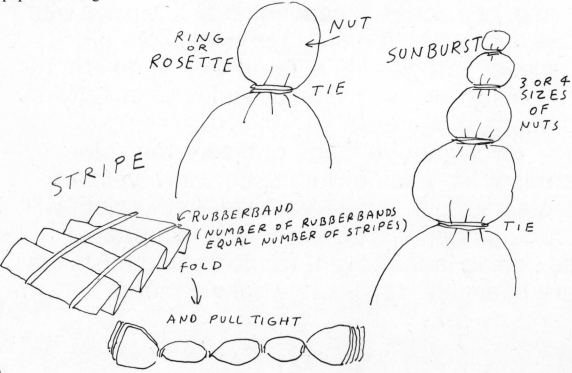

BEANBAG BUGS

9-by-10-inch paper
pencil
scraps of fabric
scissors
pins, thread
1 lb. dried beans
buttons
ribbon

Fold piece of 9-by-10-inch paper in half and draw half of the bug or butterfly. Unfold for symmetrical pattern.
To make bug, place two pieces of fabric with right sides together and pin pattern over them. Cut out.
Stitch around edges, leaving openings for stuffing on each wing, then turn to right side. Stitch along center backbone to separate wings, then fill each wing with beans. Stitch openings closed.
Trim with button eyes and ribbon feelers.

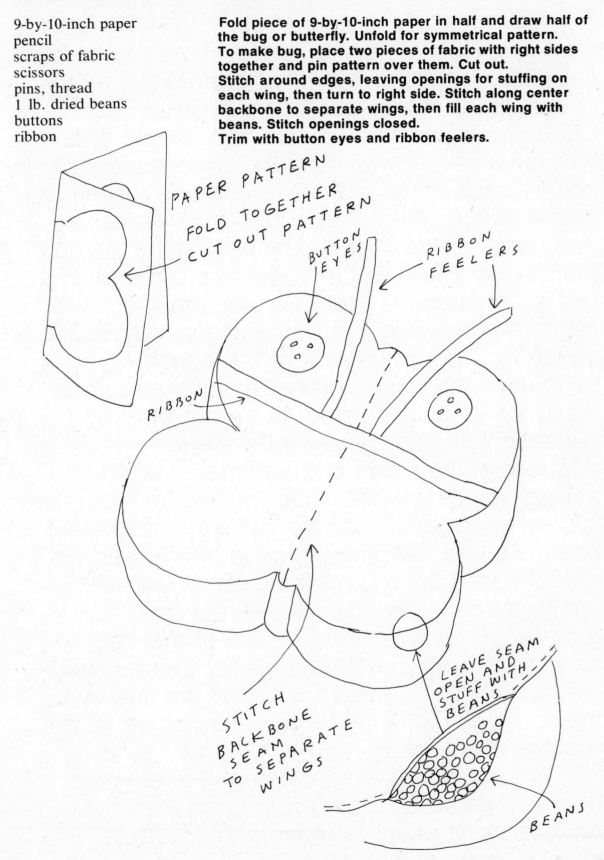

PAPER PATTERN
FOLD TOGETHER
CUT OUT PATTERN

BUTTON EYES

RIBBON FEELERS

RIBBON

STITCH BACKBONE SEAM TO SEPARATE WINGS

LEAVE SEAM OPEN AND STUFF WITH BEANS

BEANS

PASTA

Somewhere out there is a very knowledgeable man who calls himself a "Pasta Expert" and he can explain the whys and wherefores of every one of those marvelous pasta shapes. He probably knows why wheels are wheels and why bowties are what they are, and he probably knows each of the real Italian names for every single shape. We haven't met him. Maybe we don't want to. He might take some of the fun out of it for us. Pasta is fun. We have a friend who has a very beautiful and very expensive mirror frame made entirely out of sensationally exotic seashells—real, right-out-of-the-ocean seashells. We have a very beautiful and very inexpensive mirror frame made out of sensationally exotic seashells—real, right-out-of-the-pasta-box seashells. We're not saying there's no difference, but we love ours a lot. We also made a candle globe out of stacked pasta wheels that pleased us to death, and we thought we'd done something really unique. So far, three people who have seen it have remarked that it reminded them of their pet project from way back in summer camp. Well, we still love ours, even if it wasn't the first ever made. If you didn't get to go to camp, we've got a project for you.

Our kitchen has something like forty-two boxes of different shaped pasta on the shelf. And we don't even eat spaghetti! Pasta is kitchen crafts at its best.

SEASHELL MIRROR FRAME

TO MAKE CARDBOARD BACKING:

1 piece of corrugated card-
    board, 12 by 12 inches
utility or mat knife
pencil
straightedge ruler
glossy white spray enamel

Measure off points 3½ inches from each corner on
cardboard square (points A, B, C, D, E, F, G, H). Connect
points across corners (A to H, etc.) to form outer corner
edges. To find inside edge, draw lines from A to F, etc.,
parallel to each outer edge. To cut off inner corners,
draw diagonal lines from points A to D, etc. Place ruler on
lines that form shape and cut with mat knife.
Spray glossy white and let dry.

TO DECORATE WITH PASTA:

pasta: small, medium, and
    large shells, spaghetti
    twists
white household glue
mat knife

To apply pasta, dab glue on cardboard. For outer- and
inner-side edges, glue on lengths of spaghetti twists,
precut to fit. For perfection, match twist ends at each
corner to provide continuous link. Begin decoration of
flat surface along edges of smallest shells. Next place
eight to ten jumbo shells in somewhat random fashion
around center area of frame. Follow with overlapped
layers of various sized shells until cardboard frame is
completely covered. Shells should be piled extra high
toward the center portion of frame for best effect.
Allow to dry thoroughly.
OPTIONAL: For a more durable surface, brush on shellac
solution (p. 22) before painting, and allow to dry.
Spray with glossy white enamel to cover.

TO ADD MIRROR:

1 mirror 6 by 6 inches
tape picture hooks

Glue mirror to back.
Hang with tape picture hooks.

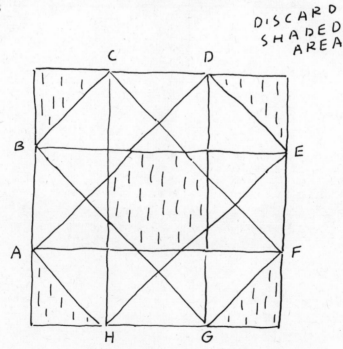

DISCARD SHADED AREA

HURRICANE GLOBE OF PASTA WHEELS

1-lb. box pasta wheels
white household glue
coffee can (for guide)
clear spray enamel
candle on small saucer

For first row, using cylindrical container as a guide, glue ring of wheels on edge in circle. Continually rotate pasta-shell globe around container to avoid sticking. Since each wheel varies in shape (not always a true circle), select the piece to fit the shape, as though you were doing a jigsaw puzzle. For second row, balance and glue wheels between wheels of first row, making alternating pattern of circles. Continue building in this way until cylinder is about 10½ inches high. Don't worry about uneven, fluctuating surface. It looks more natural that way.
Spray on clear protective coating.
Place globe over candle.

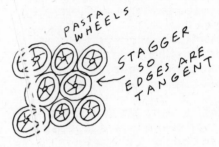

PASTA WHEELS
STAGGER SO EDGES ARE TANGENT

SEASHELL BOX

wooden box (from cigar shop
  or hobby store)
white shellac
denatured alcohol
mixing jar
brush
pasta: small, medium,
  and large shells
white household glue
tempera or watercolor paints
brush
water
paper mixing cups
clear varnish
turpentine to clean brush

Apply protective finish to box by brushing on a solution of 1 part white shellac, 1 part denatured alcohol. Allow to dry.
To apply pasta, dab on glue. Start borders around each edge with row of smallest available shells. Follow with overlapped layers of various sized shells until entire box is completely covered. Lid should be piled extra high for best effect. Dry overnight.
When glue is thoroughly dry, tint shells lightly with tan, brown, and coral paints thinned with water to duplicate natural seashell coloring. Allow some of the original pasta color to show through paint glaze. Allow to dry.
Brush on clear varnish. Allow to dry.
For variation, fill glass lamp base or glass kitchen container with color-tinted pasta shells, sprayed with clear enamel for protective coating.

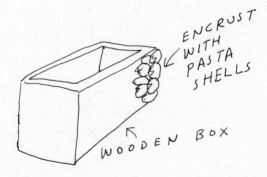

ENCRUST WITH PASTA SHELLS

WOODEN BOX

PASTA LOG CABIN

pasta:
> 2 strips of lasagna,
>> each 2¼ by 4 inches
> straight ziti, ⅜ inch in
>> diameter, cut as follows:
>>> twenty 2-inch lengths
>>> eleven 3⅝-inch lengths
>>> seven 1¼-inch lengths
>>> seven ⅞-inch lengths
>>> four 1½-inch lengths
>>> four 1⅛-inch lengths
> straight ziti, ⅜ inch in
>> diameter, with ends cut
>> diagonally inward to
>> allow for roof slope
>> (measure long tip to long
>> tip), as follows:
>>> two 2¼-inch lengths
>>> two 1¾-inch lengths
>>> two 2⅛-inch lengths
>>> two 1¼-inch lengths
>>> two ¾-inch lengths
> 1 piece ribbed jumbo elbow
>> (moderate bow to elbow)

single-edge razor blade
white household glue
clear enamel or plastic spray

House is constructed log-cabin style by layering ziti "logs" on top of one another. Actually, pasta cuts quite easily if you are careful. It's also cheap; so if you're not careful, you can do it over.

At each corner, alternate layers should overlap or butt against each other. To start, lay out rectangle with two 3⅝-inch-long and two 2-inch-long ziti. For each side, one end should butt, and one end should be butted against. Glue to hold. Repeat with same size lengths for three more layers, alternating between butting and overlaying at each corner for each layer.

To allow for window in back wall of house, shift to 1⅛-inch lengths and 1½-inch lengths on either side of centered 1-inch window opening. Make window four layers high, then complete back wall with three layers of 3⅝-inch lengths.

To allow for door in front wall, shift to 1¼-inch lengths and ⅞-inch lengths. Make door seven layers high. Turn piece upside down. This is the basic house frame.

To allow for slant of roof, stack five lengths of diagonally cut ziti on top of each end wall. (Pieces should form one continuous slant from 2¼ inches to ¾ inch at peak of roof.

Glue on two strips of lasagna for roof. Add jumbo elbow to center of back roof for chimney. Paint if desired. Spray on protective coating.

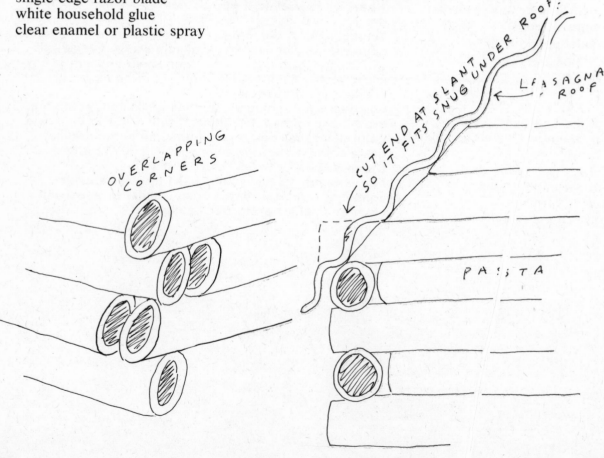

OVERLAPPING CORNERS

CUT END AT SLANT SO IT FITS SNUG UNDER ROOF

LASAGNA ROOF

PASTA

PASTA PRINTING

pasta: ribbed jumbo elbow
   for circles, wheels for
   spoked wheels
corks
white household glue
tempera paints
sponges
paper napkins
paper

To make pasta stamp, glue wheel to cork end and allow to dry. Elbow ends may be printed as they are.
To make stamp pad, dab paint on sponge. Use separate sponge for each color.
To print, press pasta stamp on sponge stamp pad and press down on paper padded beneath with napkins. Allow to dry.

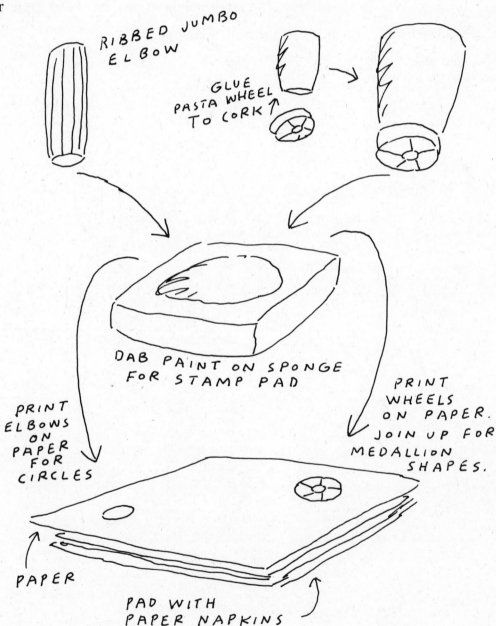

RIBBED JUMBO ELBOW

GLUE PASTA WHEEL TO CORK

DAB PAINT ON SPONGE FOR STAMP PAD

PRINT ELBOWS ON PAPER FOR CIRCLES

PRINT WHEELS ON PAPER. JOIN UP FOR MEDALLION SHAPES.

PAPER

PAD WITH PAPER NAPKINS

PASTA ROPES AND NECKLACES

pasta: wheels, ribbed elbows,
   ziti, ditali, etc. (Any
   pasta with holes can be
   used for stringing.)
thread or string
needle
watercolor or
   spray enamel paints
brush
white household glue
clear enamel or plastic spray

**Paint pasta shapes, if color is desired. Allow to dry.
With needle and thread or string, string pasta,
alternating large and small shapes.
Pendants to be hung from necklaces can be painted and
constructed separately and then tied on. Link ditali, a
spiral, and a wheel with string and glue, then add to
necklace. The more pendants, the more elaborate the
piece.
Spray on protective coating.**

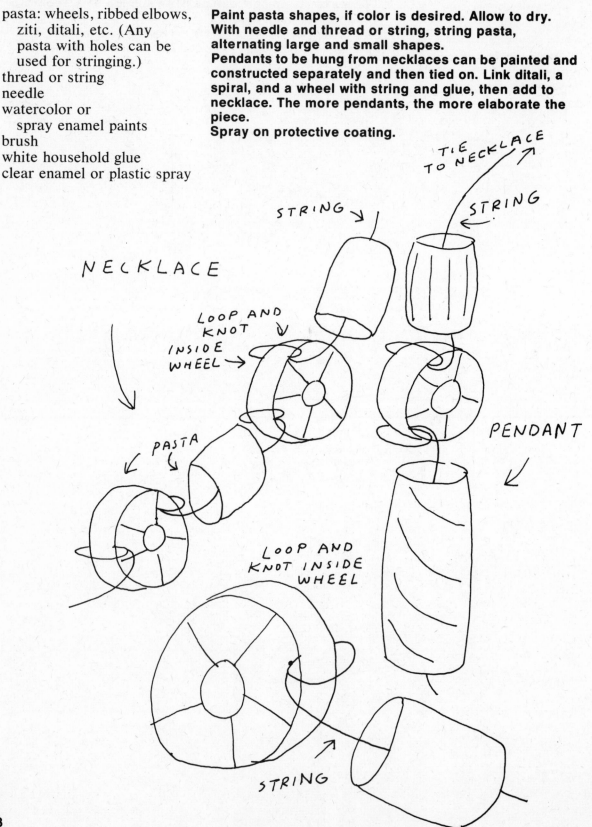

NECKLACE

STRING

TIE TO NECKLACE

STRING

LOOP AND KNOT INSIDE WHEEL

PASTA

PENDANT

LOOP AND KNOT INSIDE WHEEL

STRING

PASTA ORNAMENTS

PASTA TREE
pasta: wheels, ditali
white household glue
string

Glue three rows of wheels into flat pyramid shape. Add ditali stem.
Add string to hang.

BUGS AND BUTTERFLIES
pasta: bows, cavatelli,
  ribbed jumbo elbows,
  spirals, spaghetti
white household glue

Glue bows (wings) to cavatelli, elbows, or spiral body.
Add spaghetti scraps for feelers.

SNAIL
pasta: medium or large shell,
  spiral, acini pepe,
  spaghetti
white household glue

Glue spiral body under shell, allowing part of spiral to show as snail head. Add acini-pepe eyes, spaghetti feelers.

ANGEL
pasta: small shell, bow,
  wheel
hazelnut
white household glue
felt-tip pen
string

Glue bow (angel wings) to hazelnut body. Glue shell (head) to top of nut. Allow to dry. Add wheel (halo) to top of head. Add facial details to shell with felt-tip pen.
Hang through halo.

SNOWFLAKE
pasta: wheels, soup pasta
white household glue
string

Glue wheels and soup pasta in medallion shapes. Allow to dry.
Hang through wheel.

FLOWER BUDS
pasta: spirals, bows, shells,
  cavatelli, spaghetti
white household glue

Glue spaghetti stems to various pasta shapes to form dried buds or pods.

TO FINISH:

tempera, watercolor, or
  enamel paints
brush
clear enamel or plastic spray

Leave natural pasta color. Or paint dried pasta ornaments. Allow to dry.
Spray on clear protective coating.

CANDLES AND WAX

When you start getting into crafts involving wax, you are getting into some fairly complex stuff. People write thick books on nothing but poured candles. The same for batik. And wax casting is a whole business unto itself. You can really get involved in some difficult processes.

That's not our intent. There just isn't room enough to go beyond certain basic steps. But you'll learn the essentials with what we'll tell you. You'll be able to make candles, batik, and wax castings. And you should know enough to move on to the tougher variations. To a professional candlemaker, the melt-down-the-old, pour-out-the-new, milk-carton candle may be just a little too simple. But we love them. And after you've made a couple, you should have a pretty fair idea of how to wick and pour a candle. Making your own wax is a bit more complex, but we'll tell you how, for the time when you want to go beyond your used candle supply.

In the chapter on eggs, we touched on the batik process as the basic step in Pysanky egg dyeing. We'll get into it in a little more depth here.

When I was very little, there was a bowl of wax fruit on our table, and I remember the apple had a set of teeth marks in it. Undoubtedly some probably very small person had left behind his impressions of the realness of the cast. Making wax fruit involves a fairly simple technique with delicious-looking results. As we did with egg tempera, we'll pass on a couple of bonus thoughts on encaustic painting to put this chapter to bed.

ABOUT CANDLEMAKING

When writing about candlemaking, we found that we were continually faced with a choice between the easy way and the more complex, professional approach. In almost every case, we opted for the easy. The basics come through best that way.

Option number one has to do with how to get your wax. Either you hoard all your old candle stubs for melting down at the moment of candlemaking or, as a purist, you prepare your own wax from scratch, using household paraffin, stearic acid, and beeswax. Forget whatever you've read about using paraffin alone. It sticks in the molds, it smokes too much, it burns too fast, and it drips like a bad faucet. Some druggists, and most hobby shops, sell stearic acid. It eliminates all the awful things that happen when paraffin is used by itself. Beeswax is for beauty and a superhard finish. It's optional for most candles. Proportions of paraffin to stearic acid vary all over the lot but in our recipe, we've used a tablespoon of acid for each pound of wax and that seems to work out fine. One thing you must keep in mind at all times is that wax is highly inflammable, so it should *never* be melted over direct heat. If you should start a fire, smother it with baking soda, and cover the wax with a lid. Water will only spread the flame. Just be careful. That stuff is very hot.

As for wicks, there are also several approaches to them. You can buy prepared wicks at most hobby shops. That's easiest. Or you can melt down a real store-bought, full-length candle and fish out the wick for your creation. Or you can prepare your own. We've got a recipe for that. Another consideration too sophisticated to really get into is that the diameter of the wick should vary with the size of the candle. For now, forget that. Use what's available.

Having said all this about preparing wax and wicks, we must tell you it's easiest to melt down the old stubs the way we used to, when our creative reach never exceeded our grasp of the milk-carton technique. For your sake, we're more interested in how the candle comes out than in how it got there. But that's your option.

When molding the candle you should keep a couple of things in mind. Most important, you've got to be able to get the candle out of the mold. Unless you're using hobby-store molds that are designed to break apart, be sure you can either tear your mold apart or that there are no indentations in the mold that will keep the candle from sliding out once it's hardened. Along the same lines, the mold should either be straight or tapered outwards. Metal tart molds work exceedingly well for that reason. By the way, if you're going to use something like a milk carton, you should reinforce it with tape around the middle to keep it from sagging.

As a final option, wicks can be inserted in a couple of ways. Either string the wick through a hole in the bottom of the mold and then fasten it at the top; or pour the candle wickless, and then bore a hole through the hardened wax with a hot ice pick. If you put the wick in first, you should plug the hole at the bottom of the mold with clay or a big wick knot, and then draw the wick up through the center point of the mold and secure it snugly with a stick or pencil across the top of the mold. If you use the ice pick, you've got to fill in the hole with more wax after the wick's been pushed into the hole. Either way works. With milk cartons and such, where a hole can be pierced, the wick-first approach is good. With pastry molds and such, where there's no hole in the mold, you've got to use the ice-pick technique.

This may seem a touch naive, but basically that's candlemaking. The rest is really so much icing on the cake. The books devoted to the craft are loaded with that kind of thing.

Have fun. And be careful. Once again, that stuff is very, very hot.

TO MAKE CANDLES

TO PREPARE WAX:

collection of old candle stubs
   or paraffin, stearic acid,
   and beeswax (optional)
colored crayons
coffee cans
large pan
candy thermometer
baking soda
pan lids

Read "About Candlemaking" (pp. 82-84).
Place candle stubs or small chunks of paraffin in a coffee-can melting pot. Set can in pan partly filled with water. Using candy thermometer as guide, melt wax over medium heat until it reaches 180 degrees. If you are using paraffin, add 1 tbl. stearic acid for each pound of wax when melted wax reaches 180 degrees. Stir.
Add selected crayons to color. If several colors are to be used, individual pots for each color should be prepared. Keep baking soda and pan lids handy in case of fire.

TO PREPARE WICK:

6 yards soft white string
2 tbl. salt
4 tbl. borax
2 cups water
pan

Soak string in solution for two hours. Dip wick once in wax before using.

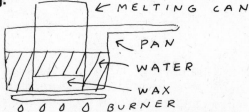

TO MOLD CANDLES:

candle mold (milk carton,
   Quaker Oats cannister,
   cardboard tubing, etc.)
can of melted wax in pan of
   hot water
wick
ice pick
modeling clay
pencil
vegetable oil

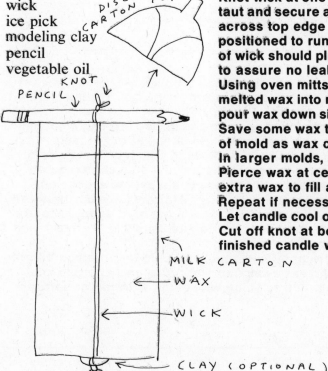

Prewaxed cartons need no coating. All others should be lightly coated with oil. Pierce small hole in center of bottom of mold with ice pick. If milk carton is used, cut off folded top of carton. If tubing is used as mold, a cardboard bottom should be constructed and taped into place. Reinforce cartons with tape around middle to prevent bulging.
Knot wick at one end and thread through hole. Pull wick taut and secure at top of mold by tying to pencil balanced across top edge of mold. Wick must be taut and positioned to run through center of mold. Knot at bottom of wick should plug hole, but modeling clay can be used to assure no leakage.
Using oven mitts to hold hot wax pot, carefully pour melted wax into mold. To avoid air bubbles, tilt mold and pour wax down sides. Fill mold to about 1 inch below top. Save some wax to fill in depression that forms at center of mold as wax cools.
In larger molds, shrinkage occurs after first half hour. Pierce wax at center of mold with ice pick, and pour in extra wax to fill any cavities that may have formed. Repeat if necessary.
Let candle cool overnight. Strip mold away from candle. Cut off knot at bottom of mold. Trim wick. Gently buff finished candle with nylon stocking.

METAL-MOLD CANDLE

TO MOLD CANDLE:

can of wax, melted over
   hot water
metal candle mold (gelatin
   mold, tart mold, etc.)
vegetable oil
roasting pan
water
ice pick

Read "About Candlemaking" (pp. 82-84).
Lightly coat all metal molds with oil to assure easy release. Fill roasting pan with warm water about 1 inch below top of mold. This bath will be used to gradually cool the candle. Set aside.
Warm mold in low oven. Using oven mitts to hold hot wax pot, carefully pour melted wax into mold. To avoid air bubbles, tilt mold and pour wax down side. Fill mold to about 1 inch from top. Save some wax to fill in depression that forms in center of mold as wax cools. Carefully set mold in warm water bath.
In larger molds, shrinkage will occur after first half hour. Pierce wax at center of mold with ice pick, and pour in extra wax to fill any cavities that may have formed. Repeat if necessary. After extra wax sets, remove candle from bath and allow to cool overnight. If candle resists release, place mold in bath of hot water and try again. Gently buff finished candle with nylon stocking.

TO INSTALL WICK:

molded candle
prepared wick
ice pick
hot wax

Remove cold candle from mold. Heat ice pick over flame and carefully bore a hole in middle of candle. Be gentle. If candle resists, heat pick again. Continue until hole is bored almost through candle. Insert wick into hole. Pour hot wax into hole to secure wick.
Trim wick when cool.

STRIPED CANDLE

TO PREPARE WAX:

1½ lbs. assorted colors of
   melted wax in cans over
   hot water
large prewaxed container,
   such as milk carton
long wick
ice pick
pencil
masking tape
modeling clay

Read "About Candlemaking" (pp. 82-84).
Cut off top of carton. Reinforce with tape around middle to prevent bulging. Pierce small hole in center bottom of mold. Knot wick at one end and thread through hole. Pull wick taut and secure around pencil at top of mold. Plug hole with modeling clay. Pour in 1 inch of first color of melted wax. Fill depressions caused by shrinkage at each level. When first layer is almost hard, pour on second color. (If wax is allowed to cool too much between pourings, layers will not bind; if not hard enough, colors will blend.) Continue layering until mold is filled to 1 inch below top.
Cool overnight. Mold should be cold to the touch before removed. Tear away container. Cut away bottom knot. Trim wick. Buff to shine with nylon stocking or soft rag.

MELON CANDLE

TO MOLD CANDLE:

assorted colors of melted
   wax in cans over hot
   water
2 identical medium-sized
   melon-shaped gelatin
   molds
vegetable oil
roasting pan
water
ice pick
knife
wick
cookie sheet
spatula
masking tape

Read "About Candlemaking" (pp. 82-84).
Lightly coat molds with oil. Prepare cooling bath with
roasting pan and warm water. Warm molds in low oven.
Pour wax carefully into molds. If multicolors are
preferred, pour wax in layers, allowing first layer to
almost harden before pouring second color. With each
layer, pierce center of molds and fill any cavities caused
by shrinkage.
Place molds in bath. Remove after first hour and allow to
cool at room temperature. Return to bath for each layer.
Let molds cool overnight.
Remove candles from molds. Cut small groove down
center of one candle. Place wick in groove. Pour thin
sheet of wax onto cookie sheet and allow to cool. Before
wax sheet hardens, lift it from cookie sheet and lay it on
candle half with wick. Trim wax to match edges of candle.
Place second molded candle on top and position to
match. Press together and tape to secure. When binding
wax is cold, stand completed candle, wick up, on heated
cookie sheet to flatten bottom.
For variations, use gelatin molds as individual candles.
Or make differently shaped candles that can be stacked
when cold. Join with binding wax as above. Use hot ice
pick to bore wick hole through candle.

EGG CANDLE

TO MOLD CANDLE:

blown egg
wax melted over hot water
vegetable oil
wick
wooden matchstick
pan
water
shot glass
vinegar

Blow and dry egg (p. 32).
Read "About Candlemaking" (pp. 82-84).
Hole at large end of egg should be ½-inch wide to allow
for wax pouring. Rinse egg with vinegar and water. Allow
to dry. Coat inside of egg with oil to avoid sticking. Knot
wick and thread through small hole in smaller end of egg.
Secure at large opening with matchstick, being sure wick
is taut and positioned to run through center of egg.
Carefully pour in melted wax.
Place egg in shot glass and stand upright in pan of warm
water. Allow to cool. Remove egg from bath and let
harden overnight. Peel away shell. Untie wick knot. Trim
wick at larger end flush with candle surface. Trim wick to
½ inch from candle at small end.

ABOUT BATIK

Wax repels paint, dye, stains, whatever. That is the basic principle of batik. If you coat a certain area of a fabric with wax and then dip the entire piece into a dye, the waxed area will not take the dye. It will retain its original color. In actual practice, hot melted wax is applied with a brush or metal applicator on the cloth in the desired patterns. The cloth is then entirely immersed in warm or cool dye. (Hot dyes will melt the wax and destroy your design.) For a multicolored pattern, the waxing and dyeing process is repeated several times. All wax is then removed when the pattern is completed. As mentioned under Pysanky eggs (p. 39), it should be remembered that since dyes tend to be transparent, each coat will show through to the next and slightly alter the color. So first coats of dye should be lighter, progressing gradually to the darker colors.

When the dyeing process is completed, the wax can be removed by pressing the cloth between layers of absorbent papers with a hot iron. The characteristic look of batik is a crackled appearance. This comes from the cracking of the wax as the fabric is crumpled in the dye bath. The tiny hairline cracks take the dye, giving an overall coherence to the design.

TO BATIK

TO PREPARE WAX AND FABRIC:

cotton fabric (old sheet, clothing, etc.)
wax: paraffin, white candle wax, beeswax
can in pan of hot water for melting pot

Wash, dry, and press fabric first, to remove any sizing or soil. Sizing may cause uneven dyeing.
Read "About Batik" (p. 88).
For best results, mix your waxes, using one part beeswax to one part paraffin or white candle wax. Melt wax over hot water at low temperature. *Never melt wax directly over flame* as it is extremely inflammable. While working, keep wax melted but control heat so that wax doesn't become overheated. Refill water in pan occasionally as it evaporates.

TO APPLY WAX:

sheet of corrugated cardboard
thumbtacks
brushes: small Sumi brushes for delicate lines, large brush for large areas

Tack cloth to cardboard as taut as possible. Dip brush in wax and paint desired design on cloth, covering areas that are to remain original cloth color.

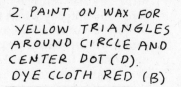

FOR REALLY CLEAR DESIGN, APPLY MELTED WAX FROM BACK SIDE OF FABRIC, TOO.

TO DYE:

batik dyes or cold water dyes (from art supply store)
large enamel pan
rubber gloves

Prepare dye bath according to manufacturer's instructions. Dip cloth in cold water, then immerse wet cloth in dye. When desired color is obtained, remove cloth, rinse away excess dye in cold water, and stretch out to dry.
Note: All dye and rinse temperatures must be cool enough not to melt wax (not over 90 degrees F.). This process of applying wax, then dyeing, can be repeated many times for as many colors as desired. In each case, the wax applied will protect the background color or the color of the previous dye.
Remove wax when the entire design is completed.

TO REMOVE WAX:

iron
ironing board
paper toweling
newspapers

Protect ironing board with newspapers. Place fabric on ironing board between layers of paper towels. Iron over the papers with iron set for cotton. The heat will melt the wax and the toweling will absorb it. Replace paper as it becomes saturated with wax. Continue until all wax is removed.
Batiked fabrics should be drycleaned.

1. SKETCH DESIGN (DOTTED LINE) IN PENCIL ON CLOTH. PAINT ON WAX FOR WHITE SPOKES (A). THEN DYE CLOTH YELLOW (B).

2. PAINT ON WAX FOR YELLOW TRIANGLES AROUND CIRCLE AND CENTER DOT (D). DYE CLOTH RED (B)

3. FINAL DESIGN WHEN WAX IS REMOVED WILL BE WHITE SPOKES, YELLOW TRIANGLES AND CENTER WITH RED-ORANGE BACK.

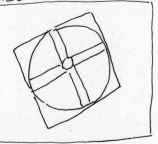

WAX COVERS AND PROTECTS COLOR OF CLOTH DYE

HAND-MOLDED WAX FRUIT

cans of wax melted over
   hot water,
crayons in assorted colors
   (purple, green or yellow
   for grapes, deep red for
   cherries, green for leaves,
   etc.)
cookie sheet
vegetable oil
wire
scissors
knife

Melt wax in cans in pan of hot water. Tint with crayons. Pour out hot wax on cookie sheet and leave until soft but warm to the touch. Coat fingers slightly with oil and roll wax into balls the size and shape of desired fruit. Insert stem wire into each ball.
Refrigerate until hard.
For grapes, twist stems together to form bunches. Pour out layer of hot green wax on cookie sheet and cut out wax leaves with knife. Press leaves to top stem of bunch to cover wires.

DECORATE ANY OF YOUR HOMEMADE OR STORE-BOUGHT CANDLES WITH THESE WAX FRUIT OR CUT OUTS.

WAX FRUIT OR VEGETABLES

TO PREPARE MOLDS:

two 1-lb. coffee cans
whole piece of fruit or
   vegetable (apple, lemon,
   grapefruit, orange, tomato,
   cucumber, gourd, etc.)
plaster of paris
4- by-12-inch strip of cardboard coated with
   melted wax
masking tape
metal straightedge or ruler
4 marbles
sand
wax melted over hot water

Fill one coffee can to the very top with fine, damp sand. Level off with straightedge to be sure can is completely filled. Press selected fruit or vegetable, stem up, halfway into sand, equidistant from edges of can. Level off sand again. Press marbles into sand at equal points between fruit and can. Bend waxed cardboard strip into a circle the size of the inside of can and tape to secure. Gently slip cardboard into sand along inside of can until the top of the fruit is about 1 inch below top rim of cardboard. Prepare second coffee can, filling it half full of plaster of paris mixed according to instructions on package.
Carefully pour plaster over fruit until it's almost level with top of cardboard strip.
After several minutes (plaster should be hard enough to give only slightly when touched), remove cast from sand. Undo tape and remove cardboard. Remove marbles and brush off any sand that may have clung to mold. If necessary, lift fruit out of mold and very carefully brush away sand inside. Return fruit to original position in mold.
Coat entire rim of mold, including marble holes, with melted wax to prevent second half of mold from sticking. Replace marbles. Wrap cardboard strip around first half of mold so that top of fruit is about 1 inch below top rim of cardboard. Tape to secure. Pour in more plaster of paris. After several minutes (plaster should give only slightly when touched), remove cardboard. Separate molds at wax point with knife and remove fruit.

TO CAST IN WAX:

wax melted over hot water
crayons
brush
knife
oil paints

Preheat molds for casting in large pan of hot water. Water should come about ½ inch below top of mold. Melt wax in can in pan of hot water and color with selected crayons to match real fruit.

Remove molds from water and carefully pat dry. Fill one mold about two-thirds full with hot wax. Fit mold together, matching marbles, and tape to secure. Rotate mold gradually to cover entire inside of mold with wax. After first two minutes of rotation, place mold under cold water and continue to turn for another two minutes. Remove tape. Remove wax fruit.

If still soft, replace mold and continue to turn under cold water until hard. Scrape off excess wax at joint. Gently buff with nylon stocking. Tint with oil paints if desired. Plaster mold may be reused.

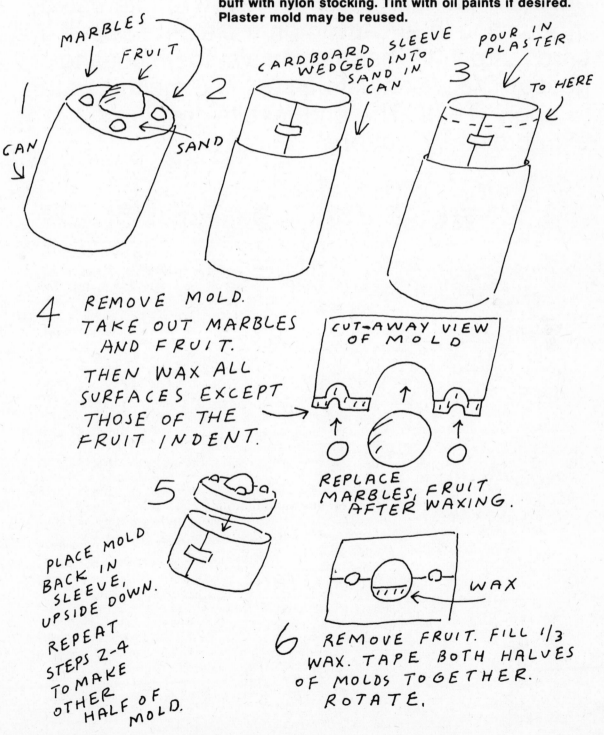

1 MARBLES, FRUIT, CAN, SAND

2 CARDBOARD SLEEVE WEDGED INTO SAND IN CAN

3 POUR IN PLASTER TO HERE

4 REMOVE MOLD. TAKE OUT MARBLES AND FRUIT. THEN WAX ALL SURFACES EXCEPT THOSE OF THE FRUIT INDENT.

CUT-AWAY VIEW OF MOLD

REPLACE MARBLES, FRUIT AFTER WAXING.

5 PLACE MOLD BACK IN SLEEVE, UPSIDE DOWN. REPEAT STEPS 2-4 TO MAKE OTHER HALF OF MOLD.

WAX

6 REMOVE FRUIT. FILL ⅓ WAX. TAPE BOTH HALVES OF MOLDS TOGETHER. ROTATE.

ABOUT ENCAUSTIC

You may never use this technique, but it's something more to know about. Encaustic, from the Greek, means "to burn." It is the process of painting with hot wax. Most of the beautiful white marble statues we now see in museums were originally painted that way. If you're interested, try painting in encaustic on a piece of board or cardboard that's been given a smooth coating of gesso. The wax must be kept in a melted state to apply. Try it. The end results are extraordinarily lustrous.

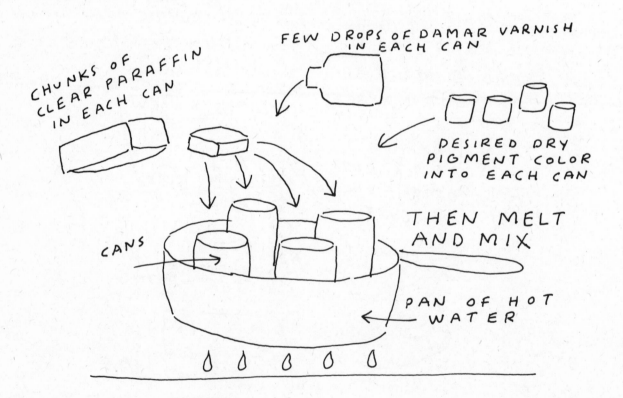

CHUNKS OF CLEAR PARAFFIN IN EACH CAN

FEW DROPS OF DAMAR VARNISH IN EACH CAN

DESIRED DRY PIGMENT COLOR INTO EACH CAN

THEN MELT AND MIX

CANS

PAN OF HOT WATER

TO PAINT WITH ENCAUSTIC

**TO PREPARE PANEL
OR CARDBOARD:**

board, or cardboard panel
gesso (from art supply store)
brush

Give surface of board or cardboard at least two coats of gesso, allowing it to dry between coats. Brush each coat in different direction. Allow to dry.

**TO PREPARE ENCAUSTIC
PAINTS:**

clear paraffin melted in cans
   in pan of hot water
dry pigment colors (from art
   supply store)
damar varnish (from art
   supply store)
sticks to mix wax

See "To Prepare Wax" (p. 85).
Add desired dry pigment color and a few drops of damar varnish to each can and heat over water. Mix well. Keep wax melted at low temperature.

TO PAINT:

melted tinted wax
brushes
lamp with exposed bulb
soft cloth
carbon tetrachloride,
   alcohol, or mineral spirits
   to clean brushes

Dip brush in wax and apply to panel in short strokes. Wax dries quickly, so there is no time for blending. Build up layers of translucent colors until picture is complete. The application is similar to that used for egg tempera (see p. 40), but final results will have a thicker, more lustrous surface.
Give finished painting final heating with a strong light bulb. This will bind it.
Polish with soft cloth.

CANS AND CONTAINERS

Now we're down to talking about the things that the basic ingredients in the rest of the book came in—the tin cans, the berry boxes, the onion sacks, and the paper bags. This is recycling at its very best. Not only do you not throw things away, you actually make objects so nice that people will be begging to take them off your hands.

A few years back you'd have been considered a touch weird if you'd gone on at any length about the loveliness of a soup can label. Now that's all Pop Art history. We've pulled together some thoughts on how to convert your prettiest labels into lapel pins, woven pillows, and even decoupage.

Tincraft is a slightly different kind of craft, somewhat more serious to its loyal practitioners. Once you get into it, you'll look forward to opening cans just so you can start slicing them up into designs.

One craft we've included may fast be becoming a victim of modern packaging. Until fairly recently, onions always came in loose mesh-string bags, just the thing for open-mesh weaving. If you keep an eye out, you should be able to find a few at local groceries. Plastic wrapping may be handy for supermarketers, but it's sometimes rough for us craftsmen.

The final recipe in the chapter is for luminarias, the paper-bag candle decorations that are used throughout the Southwest on

Christmas Eve. Their origin is Moorish, and they were introduced to the Torugas Indians by the *conquistadores.* They represent the lights that guided the Christ Child on the eve of his birth. People now use them as outside Christmas decorations along rooftops and walkways. They're a sight you can't forget.

LABEL LAPEL PIN

TO PREPARE LABEL:

label from jar or can
scissors
paper toweling
pencil
heavy paper, 6 inches square
white household glue

To remove label from jar or can, soak in water until it lifts off. Pat dry between toweling and let dry. Cut out designs of fruit, vegetable, or whatever from label, and glue on sheet of heavy paper, keeping outer shape of pin fairly simple. Press out any air bubbles and dry. Hold label up to window, and with pencil, mark areas to be raised, such as rounded fruit, on the back side of the paper.

TO MAKE RAISED SHAPES:

styrofoam scrap
rounded metal tool (melon
   scoop or measuring
   spoons)
paper cup for mixing

Wet label and place it right side down on styrofoam. Press down inside pencil lines with rounded back of melon scoop, gently rocking back and forth until shape is about ¼-inch deep. It will be raised on the right side. Continue shaping as desired. Then spread glue over back side to strengthen shaped areas.
Tear up bits of toweling and mash with a few drops of glue in paper cup. Wad this mash into backs of raised areas and dry overnight.

TO FINISH:

stiff cardboard or plastic
   meat tray from grocery
pin back from hobby shop
enamel paint
clear enamel or plastic spray

To mount label, spread glue over entire back and place on cardboard or plastic backing. Allow to dry, then cut outer shape of pin, cutting through both layers right up to edge of pictures. Glue pin backing on back of pin, with small strips of toweling glued over pin back to make it more secure.
When dry, paint back and sides. Allow to dry, then spray with clear, glossy protective coating.

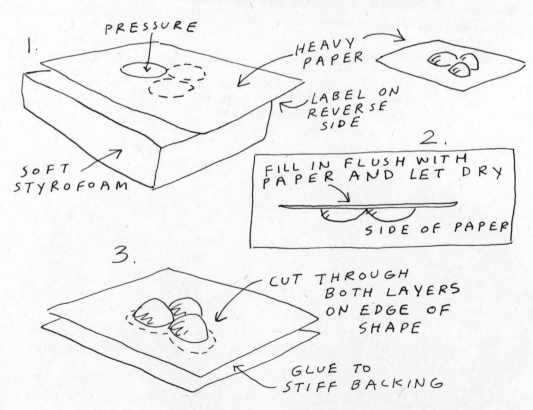

LABEL DÉCOUPAGE

TO PREPARE WOOD:

wood box or board
sandpaper, medium and fine
white shellac
denatured alcohol
wood stain
brush
#000 steel wool
jar to mix shellac

If wood is rough, sand first with medium sandpaper, then with fine. Brush on wood stain if darker finish is desired. Allow to dry. Brush on solution of one part shellac and one part alcohol. Allow to dry. Sand with fine steel wool. The surface is now ready for glueing on the cutouts.

TO APPLY CUTOUTS:

paper labels
fine scissors
shellac solution (see above)
paper toweling
white household glue
brush

Brush a coat of shellac solution on all labels (or other pictures on lightweight paper). When dry, cut out fruit, berries, and leaves. Place cutouts face down on toweling and brush glue on back. Arrange on the wood, patting out excess glue and bubbles with toweling slightly dampened with water. Allow to dry. Have as little overlapping of cutouts as possible so that surface will be even.

TO APPLY FINISH:

clear varnish
brush
jar to mix varnish
turpentine to clean brush
fine wet-dry sandpaper
fine furniture wax
soft cloth

Now the job is to bring up the surface of the wood to the level of the paper cutouts, so that the work looks inlaid rather than pasted on.
Brush on coat of shellac solution. Dry overnight, then rub down with steel wool.
Brush on coat of varnish thinned with a few drops of turpentine. Brush in one direction only. Dry at least twenty-four hours. Apply nine more coats of varnish. Then sand entire surface with fine wet/dry sandpaper dipped in water. Clean off surface and rub down with steel wool.
Continue applying more coats of varnish, using steel wool after each coat, until surface is glassy smooth and the cut-out edges cannot be felt. Four to ten more coats are usually required.
Then, with a damp cloth, apply fine furniture paste wax.

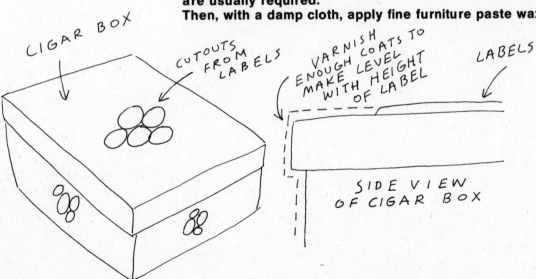

CIGAR BOX
CUTOUTS FROM LABELS
VARNISH ENOUGH COATS TO MAKE LEVEL WITH HEIGHT OF LABEL
LABELS
SIDE VIEW OF CIGAR BOX

ABOUT TINCUTTING

Old-time tinsmiths must have had some hands. Either they were a touch tougher than shoe leather or they were completely enshrouded in bandages from the wrists down. You've got to be careful. That should be our whole introduction to this craft.

We'd like to introduce you to tincutting with designs cut from tin-can lids. Besides being our favorite kind of thing, it will also give you an insight into tinworking without the problems involved in cutting open the cans, flattening them, etc. Once you've learned the routines for cutting the tops, it's an easy step to more elaborate projects using whole sides of cans. You'll need can openers, tin cutters, cans and their lids, needle-nose pliers, gloves (if you can work with them on), and patience.

And, again—do be careful.

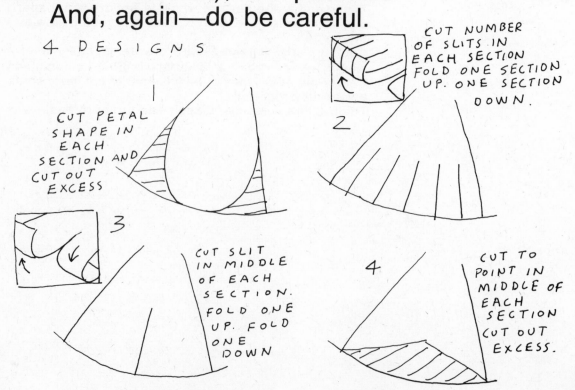

4 DESIGNS

1 — CUT PETAL SHAPE IN EACH SECTION AND CUT OUT EXCESS

2 — CUT NUMBER OF SLITS IN EACH SECTION FOLD ONE SECTION UP. ONE SECTION DOWN.

3 — CUT SLIT IN MIDDLE OF EACH SECTION. FOLD ONE UP. FOLD ONE DOWN

4 — CUT TO POINT IN MIDDLE OF EACH SECTION CUT OUT EXCESS.

MULTIPOINTED TIN STAR

tin-can lid
drawing paper
pencil
scissors
tin cutters or snips
white household glue
ice pick
thread
needle-nose pliers

With a can opener, remove lid from any size tin can. Trim rough edges with tin cutters.

Trace pattern of lid circumference on paper. Fold paper in half. Fold again into quarters. Fold again into eighths. Fold one more time into sixteenths. Crease each fold. Unfold paper circle.

With dab of glue, attach paper circle to can lid. Using creased lines as pattern, cut along each line to a point ¼-inch from the center of lid. Remove pattern. Cut V-notch ½-inch deep in outer edge of all but one of the sixteen sections. Punch small hole through sixteenth with ice pick to hang. Gently bend every other section slightly forward to create three-dimensional shape. Thread through hole and hang.

For variations, curve (petal-like), square off, or fringe fifteen sections. To fringe, make ½-inch deep cuts every 1/16 inch, along outer edge of each section. As further variation, use needle-nose pliers to twist each small fringe section upward and around plier curve.

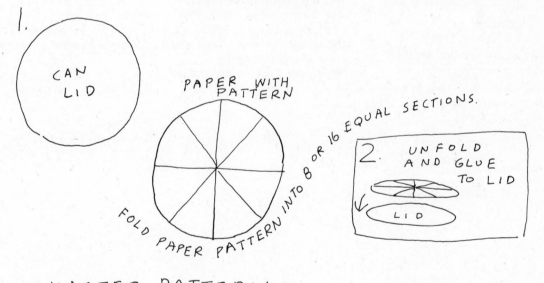

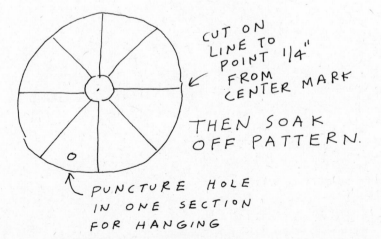

STENCILED CANNISTERS

TO PREPARE CANS:

tin cans, metal cans
    (cookie cans, cocoa cans,
    etc.)
metal primer (from hardware
    store)
brush
flat or semigloss enamel
    paints

Soak can to remove label. Peel off and allow can to dry.
Paint on metal primer. Allow to dry thoroughly.
Paint cans decorative colors. Allow to dry.

TO STENCIL:

paper doily
scissors
masking tape
enamel paint in contrasting
    color
stiff brush
small pointed brush
aluminum foil for palette
paper toweling
turpentine to clean brushes
clear enamel or plastic spray

Cut sections of doily to form border design for can. Fit,
shape, and tape in place. Holding doily steady, dab brush
with paint through doily openings. Be sure to keep your
fingers clean at all times. Continue painting until design
is complete. Remove doily, and if necessary, touch up
with small brush.
For a design variation, glue magazine picture cutouts to
can before stenciling. For a further variation,
commercially available stencils can be combined with
the doily stencils. For lettering, use alphabet stencils
from the dime store.
Spray on protective coating.

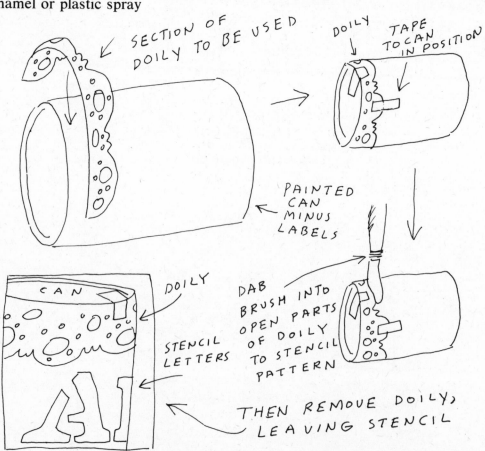

SECTION OF DOILY TO BE USED

DOILY — TAPE TO CAN IN POSITION

PAINTED CAN MINUS LABELS

DOILY

CAN

STENCIL LETTERS

DAB BRUSH INTO OPEN PARTS OF DOILY TO STENCIL PATTERN

THEN REMOVE DOILY, LEAVING STENCIL

CLOTH-COVERED CANNISTERS

metal can, any size
spray enamel paint
cotton fabric
epoxy glue
decorative edging (trim,
    braid, etc.) about two and
    a half times circumference
    of can
brushes
scissors
clear or polyurethane
    varnish
turpentine to clean brush

Spray inside of can with paint and allow to dry. Brush glue over outside of can. Cover can completely with fabric. Press out wrinkles with hands until surface is smooth and tight. Allow to dry. For large cans, glue small areas at a time because glue dries quickly. Trim fabric at top and bottom flush with can.
Brush cut ends of braid strips with glue to prevent raveling. Brush on coat of glue the width of braid around top of can. Add braid. Repeat for bottom. Trim and glue at back. Allow to dry.
Brush on clear, glossy varnish coat.
Allow to dry.
For a variation, elaborate on your use of braid by adding stripes, diagonal bands, etc., before glueing finishing braid at top and bottom.

NOTE: BE CAREFUL TO DECORATE WITH LID ON CAN SO IT WILL STILL FIT WHEN TRIM IS FINISHED.

STRIP OF BRAID COVERING ENDS →

RAW ENDS OF STRIPS

PAPER-COVERED CANNISTERS

metal can
brown spray enamel paint
brown wrapping paper or
    paper bags
scissors
ruler
epoxy glue
brown edging (gimp, braid,
    etc.)
orange shellac
brush
denatured alcohol to clean
    brush

Spray can brown both inside and out. Allow to dry.
Measure and cut brown paper into small ½-inch squares. Glue squares in rows all around outside of can. Edges should meet but not overlap. Glue edging to top and bottom of can. Allow to dry.
Brush on coat of orange shellac slightly thinned with alcohol. Allow to dry.
End result should be a mosaiclike finish for the can.

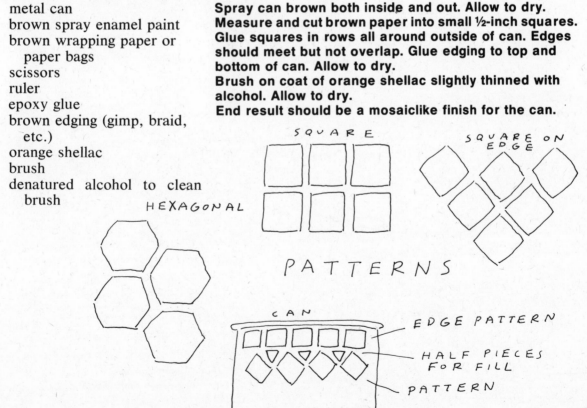

SQUARE

SQUARE ON EDGE

HEXAGONAL

PATTERNS

CAN

EDGE PATTERN

HALF PIECES FOR FILL

PATTERN

PAPIER-MACHÉ CONTAINER DOLLS

assorted containers (milk cartons, plastic bleach bottles, paper cups, coffee cans, oatmeal cylinders, etc.)
masking tape
scissors
newspaper
flour paste (see p. 7)
poster or tempera paints
brushes
scraps (fabric, paper, lace, buttons, etc.)
white household glue
string

Read "About Papier-Maché" (p. 6).
Arrange containers to form body, and tape on wadded and taped ball of newspaper for head, rolled and taped newspaper for arms. Tape doll together securely, then coat with flour-paste-saturated newspaper strips.
For hair, dip string in flour paste, and with a few dabs of glue on the scalp, arrange hairstyle, leaving ends longer than desired in finished doll; when dry, trim the ends to desired length with scissors.
Allow to dry a few days, then paint with poster paints.
Glue on scraps of lace, cloth, etc., to dress.
For small hanging dolls: Tie thread or string around neck and then knot ends for hanging loop. Hide string under glued-on lace or trim.

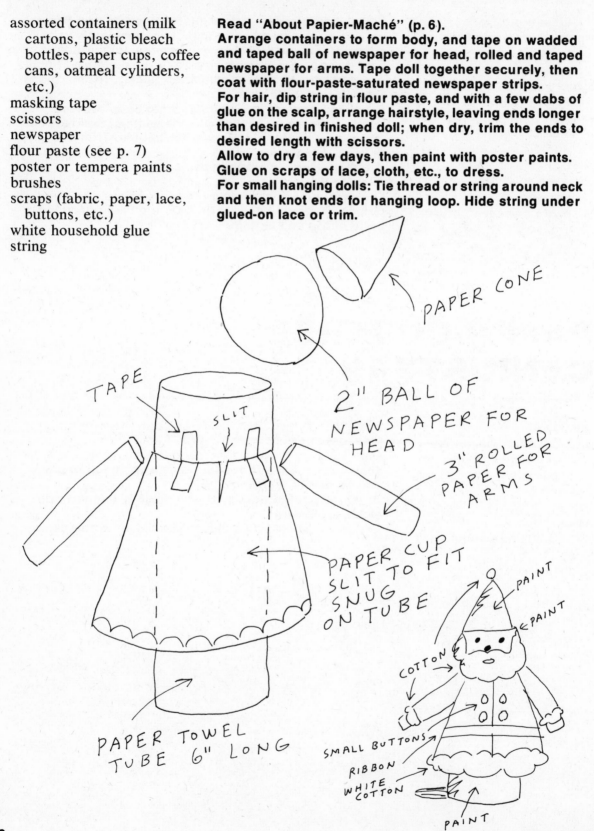

PAPER CONE

TAPE

SLIT

2" BALL OF NEWSPAPER FOR HEAD

3" ROLLED PAPER FOR ARMS

PAPER CUP SLIT TO FIT SNUG ON TUBE

PAPER TOWEL TUBE 6" LONG

PAINT
PAINT
COTTON
SMALL BUTTONS
RIBBON
WHITE COTTON
PAINT

BERIBBONED BERRY BASKET

1 square plastic berry box
   with large mesh openings
1 piece medium-weight wire
   17 inches long
ribbon: width to fit hori-
   zontal openings of basket;
   length to completely
   weave around four sides
   of basket

Twist wire ends around center of opposite sides of basket to form arched wire handle. Starting at handle base, begin to weave ribbon into and around basket, leaving about 15 inches loose end for covering wire handle. Weave ribbon in and out of basket openings and bring out at opposite handle base. Leave 15 inches loose ribbon end. Weave second ribbon around other top side same way, leaving 15 inches loose ribbon at both ends. Twist all ribbon ends up and around both sides of wire handle, tying loose bow at top center point. Complete basket by weaving ribbon around and into remaining basket layers. Fill basket with baker's-clay berries (p. 20), or papier-mâché fruit (p. 14).

MESHWORK PILLOW

TO DESIGN:

mesh bag or scouring cloth
indelible felt-tip pen
scissors
masking tape

Cut mesh square to desired size and tape edges to prevent raveling. Draw simple design with felt-tip pen or copy a label design.

TO WEAVE:

thick yarn in several colors
long yarn needle

Begin with small areas, weaving yarn in and out of each opening. Weave loose ends into back side. When design is filled in, weave background color.

TO STITCH PILLOW:

completed mesh square
1 piece fabric same size
   as mesh
needle and thread
any soft stuffing
pins
iron

Pin mesh square and fabric square with right sides together. Stitch around three sides. Turn to right side and press. Stuff; then stitch fourth side closed.

LUMINARIAS

8 to 10 brown paper grocery
   bags
sand
short fat candles

Fold rim of bag down two times to hold sack away from flame; then fill bottom of bag with about as much sand as it takes to fill a coffee can. Insert short fat candle into sand. Light.

FOLD RIM OF BAG DOWN 2 TIMES

← BROWN PAPER BAG

SHORT FAT CANDLE

SAND

LEFTOVERS

This last chapter is sort of like Sunday-night supper when you bring out all kinds of tasty odds and ends that by themselves aren't quite enough to serve up as complete chapter entrees. Because there are lots of little things to mention, we're going to shift gears slightly in terms of how detailed we get on each idea. Some things, such as kitchen-string macramé, will get the full recipe treatment. But some of the others, such as soap carving (a favorite craft way back when), will merely be mentioned, and then we'll move on. That's true leftover-fashion. If you like it, enjoy it, and don't get too hung up on what's behind it all. We hope you'll find something here to enjoy.

STRING SASH

TO FORM SASH:

heavy cord cut in 2-yard
   lengths
masking tape

Arrange 2-yard lengths of cord side by side until 3-inch-wide sash is formed (number of lengths depends on thickness of cord). Tape sash together at 6-inch intervals, beginning 9 inches from end. Be sure to keep cords flat.

TO WEAVE:

embroidery floss in bright
   colors
embroidery needle
scissors

With needle and floss, stitch ½-inch-wide stripes in and out of cord and across sash at 6-inch intervals, beginning 6 inches from one end. Stitch all loose floss ends securely into cord to prevent raveling. Remove tape. Fray both ends for 6-inch fringe.

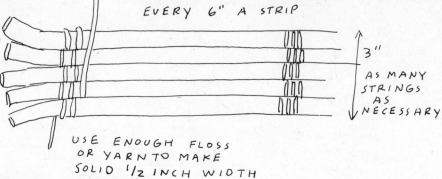

EVERY 6" A STRIP

3"

AS MANY STRINGS AS NECESSARY

USE ENOUGH FLOSS OR YARN TO MAKE SOLID ½ INCH WIDTH

STRING BOWL

ball of very thick rough
   twine
medium-size mixing bowl
white household glue
masking tape
darning needle
fine string in assorted
   colors
scissors

Using inside of mixing bowl as mold, glue and press heavy twine together into one continuous spiral. Start at bottom center and work your way up inside of mold to desired height. When desired height is reached, cut rope and glue and weave into next lower layer to finish bowl. Remove rope bowl from mold from time to time to check for openings between layers. Correct by regluing and pressing together. Use masking tape, if necessary, to hold layers together.
When rope bowl is complete, remove from mold. Allow to dry.
To decorate outside of bowl (and to strengthen sides), weave designs around individual layers of rope, using needle and fine string; needle will easily fit between layers. Connect layers with a design to strengthen.

PATTERN DETAILS

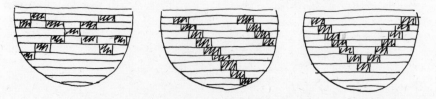

STRING-COVERED FLOWER POT

TO MAKE HANGING POT:

long lengths of strong
   cord
plastic flower pot
masking tape
scissors

To attach strings for hanging, use three or four long lengths of cord, tied at one end. Place pot on top of knot, with knot filling drainage hole. Bring cords up and tape to pot at equal intervals. Knot at top at desired length, then again for hanging loop. Cut off excess cord. Cover with glued-on stripes of varicolored string as follows:

TO COVER POT WITH STRING:

plastic flower pot
string or cord in different
   colors
epoxy glue
scissors

Turn pot upside down and, beginning at drainage hole, dab on glue; then press down spiral rows of string, changing color or tone every inch or so. When bottom is covered, hold in place with tape and allow to dry. Continue adding rows of string up the sides, glueing a few rows at a time and keeping striped effect. String should be closely packed so that pot does not show through.
Dry overnight.

SOAP CARVING

This is an old and honorable craft. I once had the pleasure of visiting the main offices of Proctor & Gamble, the makers of Ivory Soap, the *ne plus ultra* for soap carvers. In their lobby they had a full display of bars that had been carved and sent into the company. Some dated back to the twenties and very much reflected the Art Deco style of that period. They were wonderful. About all it takes is a bar of your favorite soap, a sharp penknife, and an idea that can be carved out of a bar-shaped rectangle. Animal shapes were Linda's favorites, and she tells me she was unbeatable at the craft way back when.

MATCHSTICK LOG CABIN

In the pasta chapter we gave details on how to build a log cabin out of lasagna and ziti. Wooden matchsticks with the heads cut off can be put together the same way. It's probably even easier. The only difference is that you should construct the roof out of matchsticks running vertically from the peak to the edge, rather than making a flat, lasagna-kind of thing. Take a look at page 76.

MACRAMÉ PLANT HANGER

1 jar or flower pot
eight 12-ft. lengths of
   unpolished jute string
eight 12-ft. lengths of
   white cotton string
1 plastic curtain ring,
   ¾-inch in diameter
rubberbands

Alternating between jute string and cotton twine, knot midpoints of sixteen lengths of rope around plastic ring, using lark's-head knot (diagram #1). Knot strands from adjacent lark's-head knots, using square knot (diagram #2). To avoid confusion with so many loose ends, loop individual strings around your hand, then bind each loop with rubberband. Play out string as needed.

Taking strands from adjacent square knots, tie second ring of square knots in wider circle around center ring (diagram #3). At this point, jar or pot should be positioned over center ring and used as guide for additional tyings. Pull individual sections up and around jar or pot. Hold in position with wide rubberband. Continue tying square knots up sides, using adjacent knot strings. Basket effect should be apparent.

To hold jar or pot snugly in basket, square knots at top should be tied, using double strands of jute and cotton strings.

To complete hanger, gather all strands together and tie off top ends with simple overhand knot (diagram #4). Aside from the lark's-head knot used to secure plastic ring, and the overhand knot used to tie off, all knots used are simple two-strand, or double-strand, square knots.

DIAGRAM 1   LARK'S-HEAD KNOT

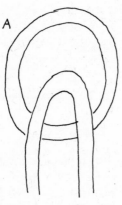

DIAGRAM 2   SQUARE KNOT

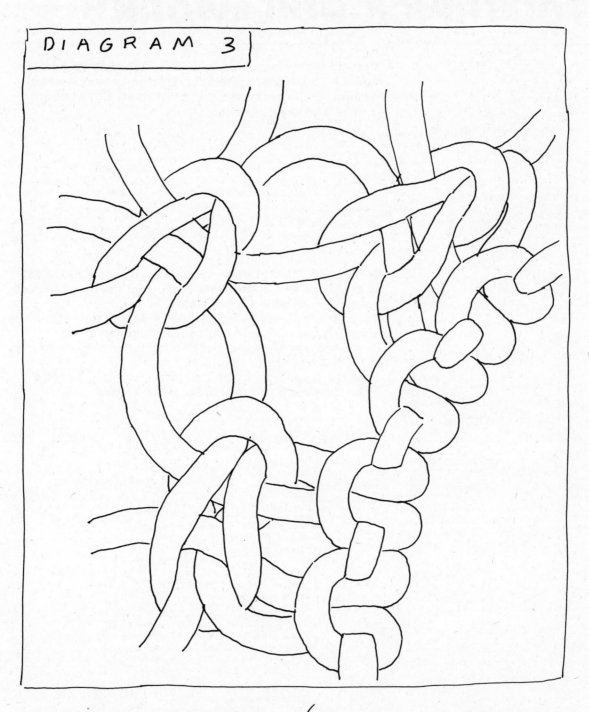

DIAGRAM 3

THIS PARTICULAR MACRAMÉ PATTERN WAS DESIGNED
BY JOHN'S BROTHER, TOM CROSS, JR., OF PITTSBURGH, PA.
AND WE THANK HIM FOR IT.

DIAGRAM 4   OVERHAND   KNOT

TOOTHPICK QUILLWORK

TO APPLY TOOTHPICKS:

object to be covered with
toothpick mosaic (any flat-
surfaced object will do:
cardboard, wood, boxes,
etc.)
wooden toothpicks
white household glue
utility knife or single-
edge razor blade

Working on a small area at a time, dab glue on surface,
then lay on rows of toothpicks. Design is best worked
in repeated patterns of squares or rows. Cover entire
surface and dry overnight.

WATERED DOWN
WHITE PAINT

TOOTHPICKS

WATERED BLACK
PAINT TO TIP OF
EACH TOOTHPICK

TO PAINT:

tempera paints: white,
red, black
brushes
paper cups to mix paints
water
masking tape
clear enamel, plastic spray,
clear, or polyurethane varnish
brush
turpentine to wash brush

Brush on coating of white paint thinned with water. Allow
to dry. Then brush the ends of the toothpicks with black
paint thinned with a lot of water. Allow to dry.
To overlay painted designs, make masking tape stencil by
pressing tape strips down over toothpicks to form
diamonds, squares, etc. Brush on paint through this tape
stencil. Allow to dry overnight.
Remove tape. Spray with protective coating, or for a
more durable finish, brush on clear varnish.

MASKING
TAPE

TOOTHPICK
SECTIONS

PAINT

TOOTHPICK
SECTIONS

PAPER-CUP SPHERE LAMPSHADE

You've probably seen those enormous ball-like lampshades made from a whole series of paper or styrofoam cups glued together. They're really quite simple to construct. You need a big supply of cups (the rimless type fit together best), masking tape, and white household glue. It's easiest to work by building three-cup triangles and then proceeding from there.

Take two cups, set them side by side with the open ends going in the same direction, and glue together along the side. Stack the third cup on top and glue it to the two-cup base. Use masking tape to hold the cups in position. Once you've got a bunch of glued and dry triangles, form the center ring of the ball by connecting triangles—one base down, the next base up—until the circle is complete. Because you've alternated the triangles, the center ring should lay flat.

Now you're ready to start building the top half. Lay the first row on top of the center ring with all triangles base down. The second row should fit in, base up. Repeat until top half of sphere is completed. Allow to dry, then complete the second half in the same way.

Leave out final triangle for bulb and socket. Wire socket to inside of frame. Unfortunately, we're craftsmen, not electricians, so you may need some outside advice on how best to handle the socket work. But that shouldn't be too much of a problem.

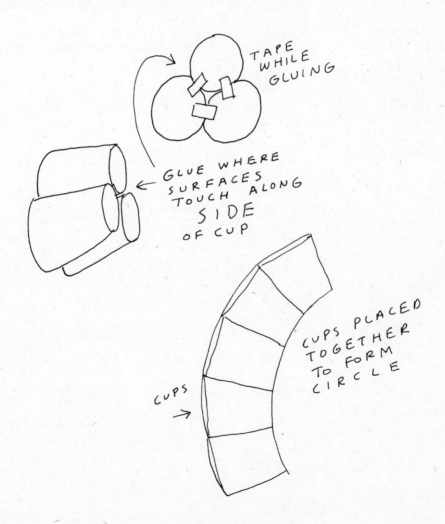

TAPE WHILE GLUING

GLUE WHERE SURFACES TOUCH ALONG SIDE OF CUP

CUPS

CUPS PLACED TOGETHER TO FORM CIRCLE

DISH-TOWEL APRON

TO MAKE PARTS:

1 dishrag, about 14 inches
  square
3 terrycloth dish towels
  about 15 by 26 inches
1 piece cotton same size as
  dishrag, for lining
1 piece cotton same size as
  dishtowel, for lining
pins
scissors
needle and thread

Combine dishrag and towel plaids or checks with
same colors.
For apron skirt, stitch two towels together, then gather
top edge.
To make sashes, cut one towel lengthwise into six strips
about 2 inches wide. Stitch two ends together to make
one long sash. Make a second long sash the same way.
Leave two short pieces for neck ties.
For linings, cut and stitch cotton sashes in same way. Pin
all sashes with right sides of toweling and cotton
together. Stitch along one long side and one end of each
sash. Reverse and press. To finish remaining long side,
turn under raw edges and topstitch.

TO ASSEMBLE:

Pin dishrag and cotton squares with right sides together,
inserting waist sashes and neck ties (see diagram).
Stitch top and both sides of squares together. Turn to
right side and press.
To attach to skirt, place top and skirt waist edges with
right sides together. Adjust gathers evenly and pin to
dishrag only, leaving lining free. Stitch skirt to dishrag
bib top and press seam.
To finish wrong side, pull cotton lining down over seam.
Fold under raw edge and pin just below seam line.
Handsew with tiny stitches.

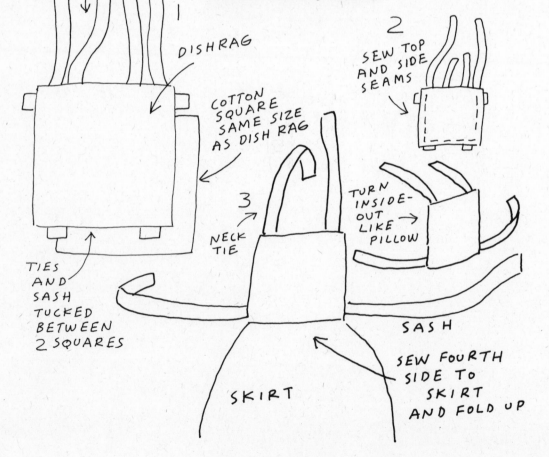

DISHRAG BLOUSE

TO MAKE PARTS:
(for medium size)

4 plaid dishrags, about
   14 inches square
2 pieces cotton, each
   4½ inches wide and same
   length as dishrags,
   for facings
pins
scissors
needle and thread

For bodice, sew three dishrags together with plaids matching. For sleeves, cut one dishrag in half.
To finish raw sleeve edges, use two pieces cotton for facings. On each facing, turn under raw edge on one long side and stitch. Then pin other side to raw edge of dishrag with right sides together. Stitch side and ends. Turn to right side and press.

TO ASSEMBLE:

2 pieces yarn 24 inches long
1 piece yarn 2 yards long
yarn needle
buttons or snaps (optional)

Place bodice flat, with one cloth for back and the other two overlapping at center front. Pin sleeves to bodice front and back, matching plaids. Try on blouse and adjust.
Topstitch sleeves and facings just under top edge of bodice with dishrag edge on top, leaving 2 inches free at sleeve edges for ruffles.
With needle, weave a 24-inch piece of yarn 2 inches in from each sleeve edge along plaid line. Gather slightly, then pull yarn to wrong side and stitch into seam to prevent raveling. Clip ends.
Weave 2-yard-long yarn sash into blouse just below bust line, using stripe of plaid as a guide. Leave ends of sash to tie at front.
Buttons or snaps may be sewn on to close front if you like.

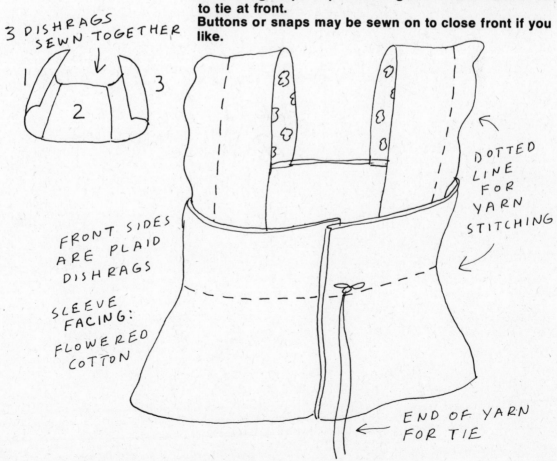

3 DISHRAGS SEWN TOGETHER

1   2   3

FRONT SIDES ARE PLAID DISHRAGS

SLEEVE FACING: FLOWERED COTTON

DOTTED LINE FOR YARN STITCHING

END OF YARN FOR TIE

GELATIN-MOLD CANDLESTICK

metal gelatin molds:
    1 large mold
    2 to 3 pairs of identical
      small molds
    1 medium cup-shaped
      mold
epoxy glue

For basic candlestick, place large mold upside down for base, then stack and glue sets of identical molds, rim to rim, to desired height. Add cup-shaped mold to top to hold candle. Allow glue to set.
For candle, see "To Make Candles" (p. 85).

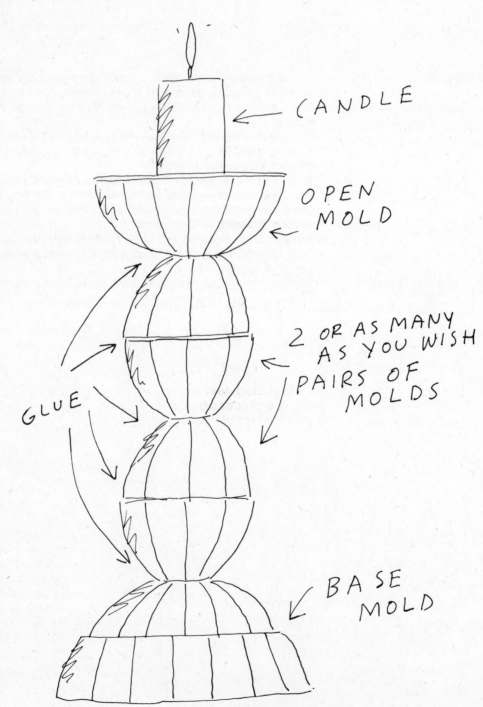

CANDLE

OPEN MOLD

GLUE

2 OR AS MANY AS YOU WISH PAIRS OF MOLDS

BASE MOLD

SPONGE PRINTING

pencil
flat sponges
scissors
tempera paints
foil pans for mixing

Lightly sketch design with pencil.
Cut sponges into shapes that can be used in many ways: an elliptical shape for leaves and flower petals, and spokes in sunburst or hex sign, and so on.
Almost any surface can be printed, but sponge printing is best used when you want to make a big picture or poster or even to decorate a wall. What you lose in sharpness of detail, you more than make up for with the ease of this technique. All that's involved is cutting sponges into the desired shapes or letters and then dipping them into paint prior to printing. The simpler the designs, the better. The more often you can repeat a design, the simpler the process. If your designs are going to overlap, let each layer dry before laying on the next.

RUBBINGS

string, can lids, matches,
    flat odds and ends, etc.
cardboard
white household glue
paper
masking tape
crayons

All items used should be about the same depth, so that crayon can move easily over paper. Arrange and glue objects on cardboard. Allow to dry.
To make rubbing, tape paper to cardboard to hold securely while rubbing. Rub back and forth with crayons, using light, even strokes, until textures and images are clear.

MAGIC TRANSFER PRINT

TO PREPARE:

pictures from newspapers,
    catalogues, funny papers,
    etc.
scissors
pencil

As a first step, test a scrap of the picture you've chosen, using the process below, to be sure the ink will transfer. Cut out selected pictures. If only small part of picture is to be used, turn picture over and outline selected part with pencil on back side. This will serve as guide during the rubbing step. Images will all be transferred in reverse, so lettering will come out backwards.

TO PRINT:

paper toweling
turpentine
smooth white paper
soft pencils
newspapers

Working on a thick stack of newspapers as padding, wet toweling with turpentine and moisten both sides of picture. Place right side of picture face down on smooth white paper. With pencil, firmly and evenly scribble on back side with close strokes. Picture must be held absolutely firm while scribbling. When back side of paper is completely blackened like carbon paper, remove picture. The result will resemble an old print, slightly faded and textured.

SUPPLIES

In line with our plans for this book, almost all the crafts materials or ingredients called for should already be sitting on your kitchen shelf. If not, they should be easily obtained through your local grocery, supermarket, hardware, or dime store.

All of the following materials are carried in most hardware stores:

aerosol spray paints
clear enamel or plastic spray fixative
denatured alcohol
dry powdered spackle
epoxy glue
fishing line
paint brushes
paint thinner
plaster of paris
polyurethane varnish
sandpaper
shellac
turpentine
varnish
white household glue
wire

If your hardware doesn't carry the following, the dimestore should:

embroidery floss
fabric trim
paper doilies
pipe cleaners
poster paint
precut stencils
ribbon
yarn

In some cases you may have to visit the local hobby shop or art supply store for a few things such as:

acrylic tempera paint
artist's brushes
artist's oil paint
beeswax
candle wicks
cold-water dye
damar varnish
dry color pigments
hobby enamel paint
jewelry mountings
oil block print color
paraffin
quality printing paper
stearic acid
textile paint

Just in case your local hobby shop or art supply store is short supplied, the following list of shops will be happy to provide you with your needs:

American Handicrafts
5947 West North Avenue
Chicago, Illinois 60639

American Handicrafts
3157 Wilshire Blvd.
Los Angeles, California 90005

American Handicrafts
508 Sixth Avenue
New York, New York 10011

Arthur Brown & Bro., Inc.
2 West 46th Street
New York, New York 10036

As a final note, we know of a few stores that deal in very specific ingredients. Their specialties and addresses follow:

Aiko's
714 North Wabash
Chicago, Illinois 60611
(batik dyes and equipment)

Aljo Manufacturing Co.
116 Prince Street
New York, New York 10012
(beeswax, cold-water dyes)

The Candle Shop
111 Christopher Street
New York, New York
(paraffin, beeswax, stearic acid,
wicks, candle molds)

Caswell-Massey Co., Ltd.
Catalogue Order Dept.
320 West 13th Street
New York, New York 10014
(floral oils, rose petals, powered gum
benzoin, gum storax, ground orris)

Fezandie & Sperrle, Inc.
103 Lafayette Street
New York, New York 10013
(cold-water dyes, dyes for fabric and
candles, dry color pigments)

P. Fioretti & Co., Inc.
1472 Lexington Avenue
New York, New York 10028
(floral oils)

Nature's Fibers
109 Tinker Street
Woodstock, New York 12498
(dyes, alum and other mordants)

Pourette Manufacturing Co.
6816 Rossevelt Way
Seattle, Washington 98115
(paraffin, stearic acid, wicks)

Straw into Gold
P.O. Box 2904-C
Oakland, California 94618
(dyes, mordants)

Surma
11 East 7th Street
New York, New York 10003
(materials for decorating Pysanky eggs)

INDEX